RAYS OF VICTORY SERIES

∞∞∞∞∞∞∞∞∞ ♦ ♦ ♦ ♦ ♦ ∞∞∞∞∞∞∞∞∞

RAYS OF VICTORY SERIES

∞∞∞∞∞∞∞∞∞ ◆ ◆ ◆ ◆ ◆ ∞∞∞∞∞∞∞∞∞

*T*his Book Belongs to:

_____

(Your Beautiful Name)

Jesus Christ in you is Greater than the spirit of racism. Let His Footprints Lead you to daily Victory over racism.

RAYS OF VICTORY SERIES

∞∞∞∞∞∞∞∞∞∞ ♦ ♦ ♦ ♦ ♦ ∞∞∞∞∞∞∞∞∞∞

150 SIGN POSTS TO VICTORY OVER RACISM

(Volume 2)

Empowering Sign Posts for Victory Over Racism

∞∞∞∞∞∞∞∞∞∞ ♦ ♦ ♦ ♦ ♦ ∞∞∞∞∞∞∞∞∞∞

Excerpts from "Nailing Racism to the Cross" Cross"

∞∞∞∞∞∞∞∞∞∞ ♦ ♦ ♦ ♦ ♦ ∞∞∞∞∞∞∞∞∞∞

Dr. Jacyee Aniagolu-Johnson

First Paperback Edition

Volume 2

Edited by Chad Steenerson (www.christianeditor.net)
Also edited by Uché Aniagolu (Ebony WoodHouse Productions)

Editing Style:
Please note that the editing style presented in this book by the second editor, Uché Aniagolu, is meant to emphasize reverence of God, His Son Jesus Christ and His Holy Spirit. This editing style may differ from what you are accustomed to, but we chose it for the reason noted above.

Cover design by Marble Tower Publishing, LLC
Cover Image Source: Online Microsoft Clip Art Gallery (Open Source)

First Paperback Edition
ISBN 978-1-937230-02-9

Printed in the United States of America by Marble Tower Publishing, LLC

Publisher's Cataloging-In-Publication Data
(Prepared by The Donohue Group, Inc.)

Aniagolu-Johnson, Jacyee.

150 sign posts to victory over racism : empowering sign posts for victory over racism : excerpts from "Nailing racism to the cross" / Jacyee Aniagolu-Johnson. -- 1st pbk. ed.

3 v. ; cm. -- (Rays of victory series)

ISBN: 978-1-937230-01-2 (v. 1)
ISBN: 978-1-937230-02-9 (v. 2)
ISBN: 978-1-937230-03-6 (v. 3)

1. Racism--Religious aspects--Christianity. 2. Spiritual warfare. 3. Christian life. I. Title. II. Title: Nailing racism to the cross.

BV4599.5.R33 A56 2011
270/.08

∞∞∞∞∞∞∞∞∞ ◆ ◆ ◆ ◆ ◆ ∞∞∞∞∞∞∞∞∞∞

"I will instruct you and teach you in the way you should go; I will guide you with My eye."

- **Psalms 32:8**

∞∞∞∞∞∞∞∞∞ ◆ ◆ ◆ ◆ ◆ ∞∞∞∞∞∞∞∞∞∞

∞∞∞∞∞∞∞∞∞∞∞ ♦ ♦ ♦ ♦ ♦ ∞∞∞∞∞∞∞∞∞∞∞

"I detest racialism because I regard it as a barbaric thing, whether it comes from a black man or a white man."

- Nelson Mandela

[Long Walk to Freedom (1995)]

∞∞∞∞∞∞∞∞∞∞∞ ♦ ♦ ♦ ♦ ♦ ∞∞∞∞∞∞∞∞∞∞∞

∞∞∞∞∞∞∞∞∞∞ ◆ ◆ ◆ ◆ ◆ ∞∞∞∞∞∞∞∞∞∞

"The truth is that in the eyes of God, our race, ethnicity or nationality does not make us either superior or inferior to anyone or group of people. Our family lineage, education, wealth, social status, influence or any other factor or distinction, does not make us better than any other family; neither will anything we own or possess as individuals make us more acceptable to God than others. All men and women, regardless of race, ethnicity or nationality, are created equal in God's excellent Image, and in humanity and dignity. This is a simple and holy truth that racism can never change."

Jacyee Aniagolu-Johnson, PhD
(Excerpt from "Rays of Victory: Nailing Racism to the Cross")

∞∞∞∞∞∞∞∞∞∞ ◆ ◆ ◆ ◆ ◆ ∞∞∞∞∞∞∞∞∞∞

∞∞∞∞∞∞∞∞∞∞∞ ◆ ◆ ◆ ◆ ◆ ∞∞∞∞∞∞∞∞∞∞∞

Dedication

This book, "150 Sign Posts to Victory Over Racism-Volume 2," is dedicated to our heavenly Father, God Almighty—a God of justice, equity and all goodness enveloped in One—our only one and true living God, who offered us all the gift of eternal salvation through His Son, our Lord and Savior Jesus Christ.

To my dear father, Justice Anthony Aniagolu and my mother Maria Aniagolu whom I love dearly and who first taught me about God, His profound love, mercy, faithfulness and grace, and His holy justice against any form of evil, wickedness, oppression and injustice.

To all those, regardless of race, ethnicity or nationality, who need God's rays of victory to deal with and overcome racial prejudice or discrimination—may your individual victory through God's beams of justice come speedily as you abide in God's Holy Word and presence through Jesus Christ.

∞∞∞∞∞∞∞∞∞∞∞ ◆ ◆ ◆ ◆ ◆ ∞∞∞∞∞∞∞∞∞∞∞

∞∞∞∞∞∞∞∞ ♦ ♦ ♦ ♦ ♦ ∞∞∞∞∞∞∞∞

Acknowledgement

My foremost gratitude is to God my Heavenly Father for His Gift of Salvation through my Lord and Savior Jesus Christ, and the power of His Holy Spirit Who dwells within me. It is He Who inspires and fuels me daily to overcome any and all challenges, including my experiences with racial prejudice and discrimination.

My deepest gratitude goes to my dad, Justice Anthony Aniagolu and my mom, Lady Maria Aniagolu, for being the most amazing parents and irreplaceable gifts from God. I will forever remain grateful to God for finding me worthy to have such phenomenal persons as mom and dad. I love always!

My special gratitude goes to my husband, Lamonte, who remains my earthly rock of Gibraltar, and through whom God continues to teach me His expression of true and unconditional love that has no bounds.

My special gratitude also goes to my sister, Maryanne, a lovely woman of God—thank you for continuing to help me to better understand how to hear the true voice of God and how to spend endless quality time in God's Holy Presence through prayer, thanksgiving and worship. I love you very much.

To my sister Uché, I thank God for the sweet fragrance of Christ in you. You are an embodiment of servanthood—selfless sacrificial giving, and it is the greatness of God in you through Jesus Christ that empowers you to humble yourself to serve others; I have no doubt that God will magnify His glory in your life through Jesus Christ. I love you very much.

To my sister Chi-Chi who's giving spirit surpasses anyone that I know—May Luke 6:38 remain like a wellspring within you and may God continue to bless you and enrich your life beyond your wildest imagination through Jesus Christ! I love you very much.

To my brother Kizito whose deep and genuine love for God helps me to stay focused on Matthew 6:33; may the power of God's Holy Word continue to promote you from faith to faith and from glory to glory, in the awesome Name of our Lord and Savior Jesus Christ. I love you very much.

To the rest of my family, Tony, Emeka, Chuka, Lolly and Nwachu, I remain forever grateful to God for your lives, individual families and accomplishments. It is my prayer that John 3:16 will be and remain alive in your hearts. I love you very much.

To my sisters in the Lord Jesus Christ, Chinwe Igwegbe-Lane, Nonye Igwegbe and Cathy Agada, thank you for all your prayers and support and powerful prophetic words that sustained me during the final birthing stage of the RAV book series. May our Heavenly Father continue to take you from faith to Faith and from glory to Glory, in the awesome Name of our Lord and Savior Jesus Christ!

To the rest of my friends, prayer partners and the Ocean of Mercy prayer group in Cork, Ireland, who prayed for the completion and success of the Rays of Victory book series, and to the Body of Jesus Christ (believers in Christ, God's true priests and ministers around the world), regardless of denomination, race, ethnicity or nationality, may God's favor and blessings always overflow in your lives as you continue to spread the good news of the Gospel of our Lord and Savior Jesus Christ, and further His powerful ministry, all of which are firmly rooted in true and pure love, which is God Himself.

∞∞∞∞∞∞∞∞∞ ◆ ◆ ◆ ◆ ◆ ∞∞∞∞∞∞∞∞∞

Contents

∞∞∞∞∞∞∞∞∞ ♦ ♦ ♦ ♦ ♦ ∞∞∞∞∞∞∞∞∞∞

What is Racism?

"A situation in which one race maintains supremacy over another race through a set of attitudes, behaviors, social structures and ideologies. It involves four essential and interconnected elements:

Power: *the capacity to make and enforce decisions is disproportionately or unfairly distributed.*

Resources: *unequal access to such resources as money, education, information, etc.*

Standards: *standards for appropriate behavior are ethnocentric, reflecting and privileging the norms and values of the dominant race or society.*

Problem: *involves defining "reality" by naming "the problem" incorrectly, and thus misplacing it."*

-- Women's Theological Center, Boston, MA, 1994

∞∞∞∞∞∞∞∞∞∞ ♦ ♦ ♦ ♦ ♦ ∞∞∞∞∞∞∞∞∞∞

∞∞∞∞∞∞∞∞∞∞ ♦ ♦ ♦ ♦ ♦ ∞∞∞∞∞∞∞∞∞∞

Definitions of Racism

"Any distinction, exclusion, restriction, or preference based on race, color, descent, or national or ethnic origin which has the purpose or effect of nullifying or impairing the recognition, enjoyment, or exercise, on equal footing, of human rights and fundamental freedoms in the political, economic, social, cultural, or any other field of public life."

-- The ICERD
(International Convention on the Elimination of All Forms of Racial Discrimination)

∞∞∞∞∞∞∞∞∞∞ ♦ ♦ ♦ ♦ ♦ ∞∞∞∞∞∞∞∞∞∞

"Racism has not disappeared... we confront forms of racism that are covert or more complex..."

-- The International Council on Human Rights Policy

∞∞∞∞∞∞∞∞∞∞ ♦ ♦ ♦ ♦ ♦ ∞∞∞∞∞∞∞∞∞∞

"Racism involves physical, psychological, spiritual, and social control, exploitation and subjection of one race by another race...This means that

racial discrimination and injustice are established, perpetuated and pro-moted throughout every institution of society - economics, education, entertainment, family, labor, law, politics, religion, science and war..."

-- Phavia Kujichagulia
(Recognizing and Resolving Racism: A Resource and
Guide for Humane Beings)

∞∞∞∞∞∞∞∞∞∞ ♦ ♦ ♦ ♦ ♦ ∞∞∞∞∞∞∞∞∞∞

"Racism - Racial prejudice and discrimination that are supported by institutional power and authority. The critical element that differentiates racism from prejudice and discrimination is the use of institution-al power and authority to support prejudices and enforce discriminatory behaviors in systematic ways with far-reaching outcomes and effects..."

-- Enid Lee, Deborah Menkart and Margo Okazawa-Rey
(eds.)
(Beyond Heroes and Holidays: A Practical Guide to K-12
Anti-Racist, Multicultural Education and Staff Develop-
ment.)

∞∞∞∞∞∞∞∞∞∞ ♦ ♦ ♦ ♦ ♦ ∞∞∞∞∞∞∞∞∞∞

∞∞∞∞∞∞∞∞∞∞∞ ♦ ♦ ♦ ♦ ♦ ∞∞∞∞∞∞∞∞∞∞∞

The Reason for this Book

For every person, every child of God to know, understand and use the awesome power of God's Holy Word and His power within him or her through Jesus Christ to slay the goliath racism that they may encounter anywhere.

"You, dear children, are from God and have overcome them, because the one who is in you is greater than the one who is in the world."
- **1 John 4:4, NIV**

∞∞∞∞∞∞∞∞∞∞∞ ♦ ♦ ♦ ♦ ♦ ∞∞∞∞∞∞∞∞∞∞∞

To receive the spirit of racism is to reject God's Holy Word.
To practice racism is to disobey God's Holy Word.
To reject the spirit of racism is to uphold God's Holy Word.

∞∞∞∞∞∞∞∞∞∞∞ ♦ ♦ ♦ ♦ ♦ ∞∞∞∞∞∞∞∞∞∞∞

∞∞∞∞∞∞∞∞∞ ♦ ♦ ♦ ♦ ♦ ∞∞∞∞∞∞∞∞∞

Preface

This book, "150 Sign Posts to Victory Over Racism-Volume 2," is a continuation of Volume 1 containing excerpts from the "Rays of Victory-Nailing Racism to the Cross" series. The goal in writing this book is to lead you to accept Jesus Christ as your personal Lord and Savior, if you have not already done so; to guide you to God's holy truth in His Holy Word by the revelation power of His Holy Spirit; and for you to understand how to submit to God's Word and allow Him to unveil your natural eyes, replacing them with spiritual eyes through Jesus Christ. With spiritual eyes you can begin to recognize the activities of the foul spirit of racism that is behind the racial prejudice and discrimination that you have experienced in the past or that you are currently experiencing. You will come to understand how racism attacks you and tries to intimidate you to submit to evil domination.

With a spiritual mindset, you will understand how to resist and defeat the obnoxious spirit of racism with God's Holy Word, the Sword of the Spirit (Ephesians 6:17). You will also understand how to be used as an instrument of God, transformed into His "battleaxe" against all demonic lies and influences, including racism (Ephesians 6:17; Jeremiah 51:20-23). God's Holy Word loaded in you also fortifies and transforms you into His battleaxe, a spiritual warrior against all forms of evil, as well as racism (Psalms 144:1-2). As God's battleaxe you cannot be a human receptacle for the evil spirit of racism or its tool for perpetrating racism, or see yourself as a victim of racism; rather you are a victorious power house of prayer, a spiritual prayer warrior over the vile spirit of racism and racist acivities it perpetrates through its willing human hosts.

The excerpts in this book are about showing you how not to submit to the obnoxious spirit of racism; rather how to apply God's Holy Word to shatter the stranglehold that racism may have on your soul—your heart, mind, thoughts, will and resolve, and on your personality, actions, and behavior. If you have already allowed the foul spirit of racism access to your soul, now is the time to cast it out. If you have not granted the evil spirit of racism any such access, keep the door to your soul permanently shut to it, with the power of the holy truth of God's awesome Word.

Are you burdened by the foul spirit of racism and cannot seem to shake it off? Do you wish to turn over a new leaf with a life that is devoid of prejudiced feelings or racist actions? Are you a member of the huge "club" of individuals who face the daily storms of racism in the workplace or elsewhere? Have you had enough of the negative spiritual, mental or even physical abuse and torture by your experiences with racism? If you have, please come with me on this powerful trip with God's Spiritual knowledge, guidance and empowerment. Let the excerpts in is book, empowering "sign posts" guide you on how to draw daily-renewed strength from God's Holy Scripture. Let the power of God's Holy Word and His amazing grace unshackle you forever from the invisible chains of racism.

Scripture Meditation

Let God battle those who oppress you—let God oppose those who oppose you—let Him be an Enemy to your enemies and an Adversary to your adversaries (Exodus 23:22) — let Him gain victory for you—the battle is not yours but the Lords'. (1 Samuel 17:45-47)

∞∞∞∞∞∞∞∞ ♦ ♦ ♦ ♦ ♦ ∞∞∞∞∞∞∞∞
♥

How to Use this Book

This book, "150 Sign Posts to Victory Over Racism-Volume 2," contains empowering guideposts for victory over racism, excerpts from the "Rays of Victory Series – Nailing Racism to the Cross."

During your quiet and serene moments, read and meditate on each excerpt, page by page, and most importantly, on God's Holy Word. To mediate means to reflect on or to contemplate; to look at attentively and thoughtfully; to consider carefully and at length or ponder; to have in mind as an intention or possibility.[1] So, like a fresh spring of water, let God's Holy Word running through the "sign posts" soak into your heart and mind and help you to begin to carve out a spiritual roadmap for you as your daily Christ-rooted strategy for gaining victory over racism. Let each excerpt help you to refocus your mind on Romans 12:2 and let the power of God Holy Word begin to renew and fortify your mind against the foul spirit of racism.

Let the excerpts in this book become to you guiding "sign posts" that lead you to draw daily-renewed strength from God's Holy Scripture, through Jesus Christ and by the revelation power of God's Holy Spirit. Let the power of God's Holy Word and His amazing grace unshackle you forever from the invisible chains and stranglehold of racism.

First, let's profess Jesus Christ as our Lord and Savior, and receive the redeeming power of His precious Blood in our individual lives. For it is under the covering of the precious Blood of Jesus that we can receive the hidden power of God's Rays of Victory over racism (Habakkuk 3:4).

♥

∞∞∞∞∞∞∞∞∞∞ ♦ ♦ ♦ ♦ ♦ ∞∞∞∞∞∞∞∞∞∞∞

Chapter Reference

1. *www.thefreedictionary.com*

∞∞∞∞∞∞∞∞∞ ♦ ♦ ♦ ♦ ∞∞∞∞∞∞∞∞∞∞
♥

A Prayer of Salvation

On this day, _____, I, _____ confess with my mouth that the Lord Jesus Christ is my personal Savior; I believe that He shed His Blood for me on the Cross of Calvary and that God raised Him from the dead for my eternal salvation. I repent of my sins and ask for God for forgiveness through the mighty Blood of Jesus Christ.

On this day, _____ by my faith, I, _____ believe that I am now saved by the precious Blood of Jesus Christ. I believe in the Triune God: God the Father, God's Son, Jesus Christ and God the Holy Spirit. I believe that in the Name of our Lord and Savior Jesus Christ, I will receive the baptism of God's Holy Spirit that will release from my heart the flowing rivers of Living Water, in Jesus' Name, Amen.

Thank you Father, Lord God, for on this day, _____, in the Name of Jesus Christ, I, _____ am Born Again!

Scripture Meditation:

"For God so loved the world that He gave His Only Begotten Son, that whoever believes in Him should not perish but have everlasting life." –
John 3:16

"But what does it say? 'The word is near you, in your mouth and in your heart' (that is, the word of faith which we preach): that if you confess with your mouth the Lord Jesus and believe in your heart that God has raised Him from the dead, you will be saved. For with the heart one believes unto righteousness, and with the mouth confession is made unto salvation." – Romans 10:8-9

"He who believes in Me, as the Scripture has said, out of his heart will flow rivers of Living Water." – John 7:38

"That which is born of the flesh is flesh, and that which is born of The Spirit is spirit. Do not marvel that I said to you, 'You must be Born Again.'" – John 3:6-7

♥

∞∞∞∞∞∞∞∞ ♦ ♦ ♦ ♦ ♦ ∞∞∞∞∞∞∞∞

Prayer after Profession of Salvation

∞∞∞∞∞∞∞∞ ♦ ♦ ♦ ♦ ♦ ∞∞∞∞∞∞∞∞

♥

Dear Glorious Heavenly Father, thank You that I am born again by the precious Blood of Jesus Christ. I accept my renewed spirit in Him.

Dear gracious Father, I thank You for making me aware that I have spiritual and mental shackles from my experiences with racism. Thank You for revealing to me all areas where I am shackled. Thank You for giving me total release and freedom from the intrigues of the foul spirit of racism. I reject the evil tradition of racism and all that it stands for. I forgive anyone who has hurt or offended me in any manner, including my racist offenders.

Dear precious Father, I believe that You have answered my prayers in the precious Name of Jesus Christ. In the Name of Jesus Christ and by Your enabling grace, Lord God, I know that I can and that I have gained victory over any form of racial oppression and injustice.

Thank You, awesome Father, for Your marvelous rays of victory over racism on my behalf, and for Your limitless and boundless power within me through Jesus Christ, Amen.

Scripture Meditation:

"And whatever you ask in My Name, I will do, that the Father may be Glorified in the Son. If you ask anything in My Name, I will do it." – John 14:13-14

"Pray without ceasing; in everything give thanks; for this is the Will of God in Jesus Christ for you." – 1 Thessalonians 5:17-18

"And whenever you stand praying, if you have anything against anyone, forgive him that your Father in Heaven may also forgive you your trespasses." – Mark 11:25

"Until now you have asked nothing in My Name. Ask and you will receive, that your joy may be full."– John 16:24

"Don't copy the behavior and customs of this world, but let God transform you into a new person by changing the way you think. Then you will learn to know God's Will for you, which is good and pleasing and perfect." – Romans 12:2

♥

∞∞∞∞∞∞∞∞∞∞ ♦ ♦ ♦ ♦ ♦ ∞∞∞∞∞∞∞∞∞∞

Partnership Prayer

∞∞∞∞∞∞∞∞∞ ◆ ◆ ◆ ◆ ∞∞∞∞∞∞∞∞∞
♥

I commit to spending quality time in prayer, worship and thanksgiving, and meditating on God's Holy Word, to receive His powerful and winning strategies for my daily victory over racism. This I shall do only by the grace of God, in the Name of our Lord and Savior Jesus Christ and through daily guidance by the Holy Spirit. I stand in agreement with my prayer partner(s) _____ believing that through the redeeming precious Blood of Jesus Christ, God has taken away the burden of racism, its reproach and yoke of destruction from all areas of my life. I stand in agreement with my prayer partner(s) _____ believing that the precious Blood of Jesus Christ has permanently destroyed and removed the power of the burden of the foul spirit of racism in my life, in Jesus' Name, Amen.

_____

Your Name

_____

Prayer Partner's Name

∞∞∞∞∞∞∞∞∞∞ ♦ ♦ ♦ ♦ ∞∞∞∞∞∞∞∞∞∞

Jacyee Aniagolu Johnson

Dr. Jacyee Aniagolu-Johnson
(Author remains in agreement with you)

"Again I say to you that if two of you agree on earth concerning anything that they ask, it will be done for them by My Father in heaven." – Matthew 18:19

"It shall come to pass in that day that his burden will be taken away from your shoulder, and his yoke from your neck, and the yoke will be destroyed because of the anointing oil." – Isaiah 10:27

♥

∞∞∞∞∞∞∞∞∞∞ ♦ ♦ ♦ ♦ ∞∞∞∞∞∞∞∞∞∞

Introduction

∞∞∞∞∞∞∞∞∞ ♦ ♦ ♦ ♦ ♦ ∞∞∞∞∞∞∞∞∞

♥

"150 Sign Posts to Victory Over Racism – Volume 2" is about empowering you to gain individual victory over racism; by you standing in the victory that Jesus Christ gained for you on the Holy Cross, where He nailed your sins and every form of evil, wickedness, injustice, and oppression, including racism.

To stand in victory over racism, you must first come under the covering of the precious Blood of our Lord and Savior, Jesus Christ. You need to accept Jesus Christ as your personal Lord and Savior. Once you have *truly* accepted Jesus Christ as your Redeemer, you are transformed into a new creation in Christ (2 Corinthians 5:17). You become "born again" in Jesus Christ (John 3:6-7, 16). To be "born again" or "reborn" in Jesus Christ does not mean a physical rebirth but a spiritual renewal of your spirit.

To gain individual victory over racism or any other form of evil; first, you must come to know and understand who you are in Jesus Christ. You are a child of God through the righteousness of Jesus Christ, an heir of God, and joint-heir with Christ (Romans 8:15-18). You are fearfully and wonderfully made, and you are an excellent product of His mar- marvelous works (Psalms 139:13-14). So, you must come to see yourself as God sees you and not as prejudiced or racist individuals see you or present you to the world. You must start to meditate on God's Holy Word and allow it to begin to renew your mind daily through Jesus Christ (Romans 12:2) so that you do not allow racism to distort your view of yourself, or control or direct your heart and mind.

If you have already allowed racism to distort your dis- cernment or perception of your image of yourself in your mind, then you need to let God's Holy Word start the process of renewing your mind and give you a brand new view of your image in your mind—your authentic image, which is your true spiritual image in Him. As a child of God, you cannot allow the foul spirit of racism to deceive you into believing the lies that racism presents to you about who you are—because rac- ism is of the devil who is the father of all lies and no truth can ever come from him (John 8:44); rather you are to veto and thrash the lies of racism, believe God's Holy Word and obey His Word and do His will (James 1:22-25).

God's will is for you to silence the foul spirit of racism with the power of His Holy Word in you. You are what God's Word says you are and not what racists declare that you are. As a child of God you have the power of God's Holy Spirit in you through Jesus Christ, to pull down every stranglehold or iron grip of racism and bring racism and its evils to submit to God's Holy Word (2 Corinthians 10:3-5).

Now, let us begin a new journey with Jesus Christ—a renewed path of authentic spiritual power, faith, love, charity, truth, faithfulness, holiness, mercy, forgiveness, and justice. Let us turn a new leaf and start a new, refreshed and fabulous journey with Him that takes us to victory over daily challenges and obstacles—and over the foul and obnoxious spirit of racism. Let us follow His holy "sign posts" to victory over racism. Let's begin!

♥

∞∞∞∞∞∞∞∞∞∞ ♦ ♦ ♦ ♦ ♦ ∞∞∞∞∞∞∞∞∞∞

"150 Sign Posts to Victory Over Racism – Volume 2" Begins:

1

The foul spirit of racism is an evil demoralizing spirit that attempts to burden and soil our soul with lies (John 8:44). Don't allow it! Reject the vile spirit of racism and its product racism!

2

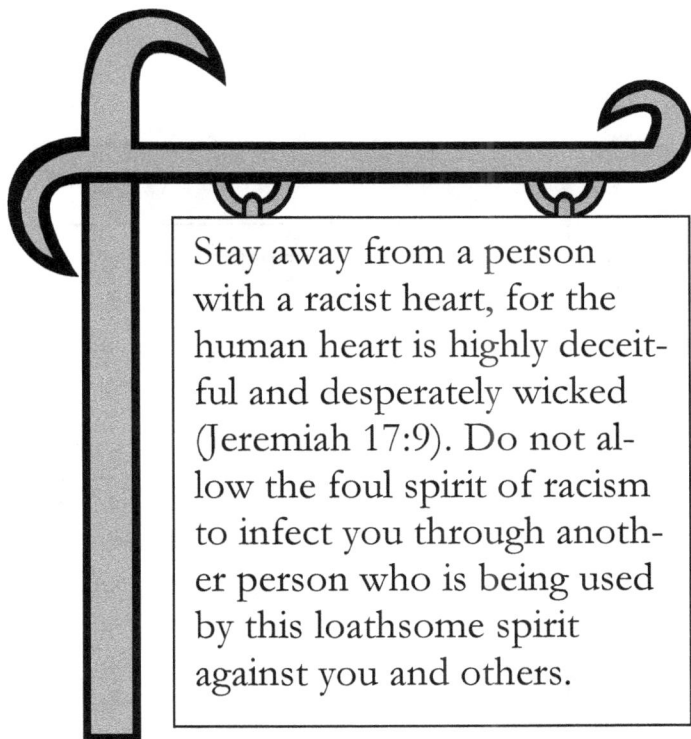

Stay away from a person with a racist heart, for the human heart is highly deceitful and desperately wicked (Jeremiah 17:9). Do not allow the foul spirit of racism to infect you through another person who is being used by this loathsome spirit against you and others.

3

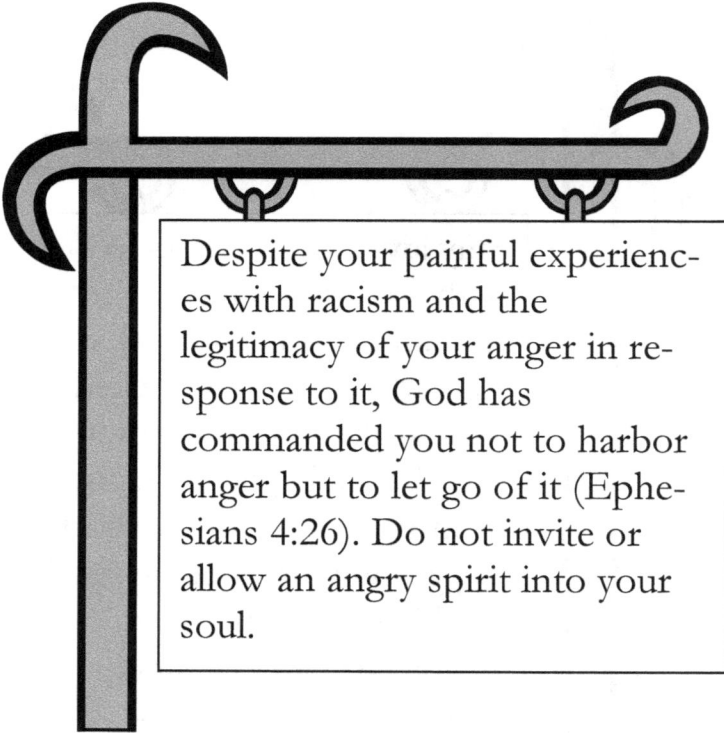

Despite your painful experiences with racism and the legitimacy of your anger in response to it, God has commanded you not to harbor anger but to let go of it (Ephesians 4:26). Do not invite or allow an angry spirit into your soul.

4

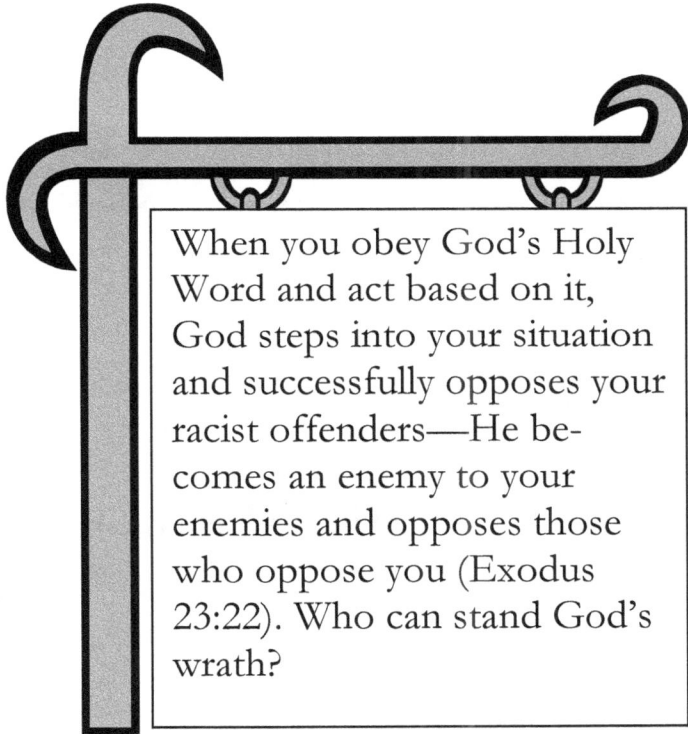

When you obey God's Holy Word and act based on it, God steps into your situation and successfully opposes your racist offenders—He becomes an enemy to your enemies and opposes those who oppose you (Exodus 23:22). Who can stand God's wrath?

5

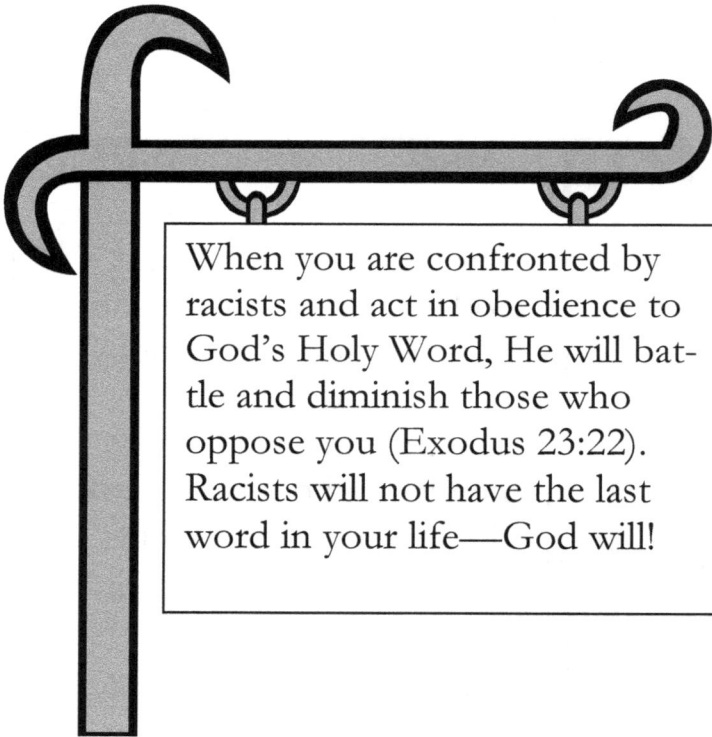

When you are confronted by racists and act in obedience to God's Holy Word, He will battle and diminish those who oppose you (Exodus 23:22). Racists will not have the last word in your life—God will!

6

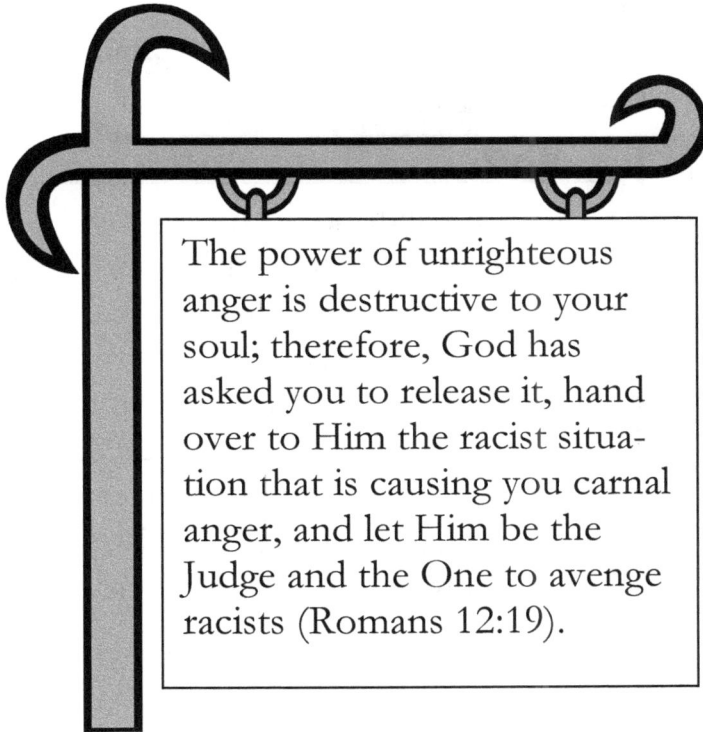

The power of unrighteous anger is destructive to your soul; therefore, God has asked you to release it, hand over to Him the racist situation that is causing you carnal anger, and let Him be the Judge and the One to avenge racists (Romans 12:19).

7

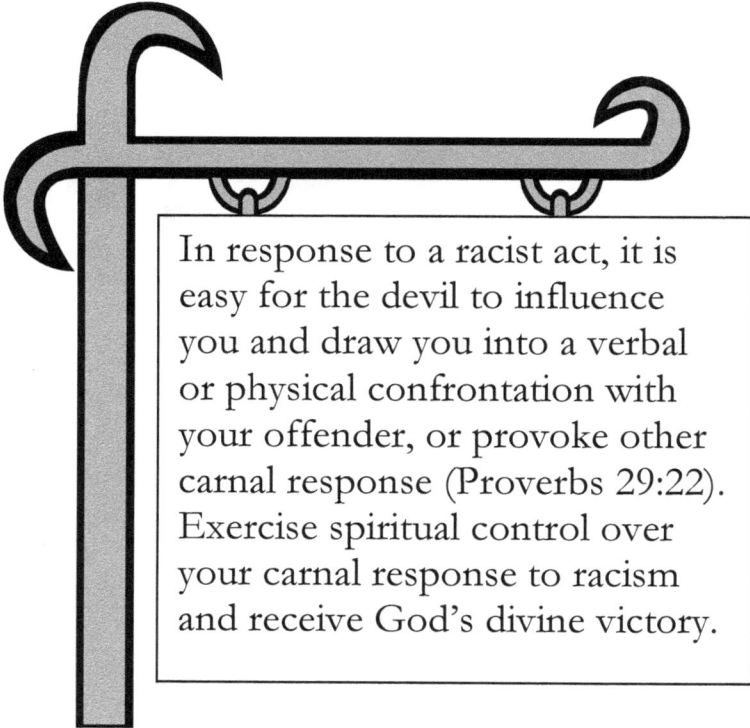

In response to a racist act, it is easy for the devil to influence you and draw you into a verbal or physical confrontation with your offender, or provoke other carnal response (Proverbs 29:22). Exercise spiritual control over your carnal response to racism and receive God's divine victory.

8

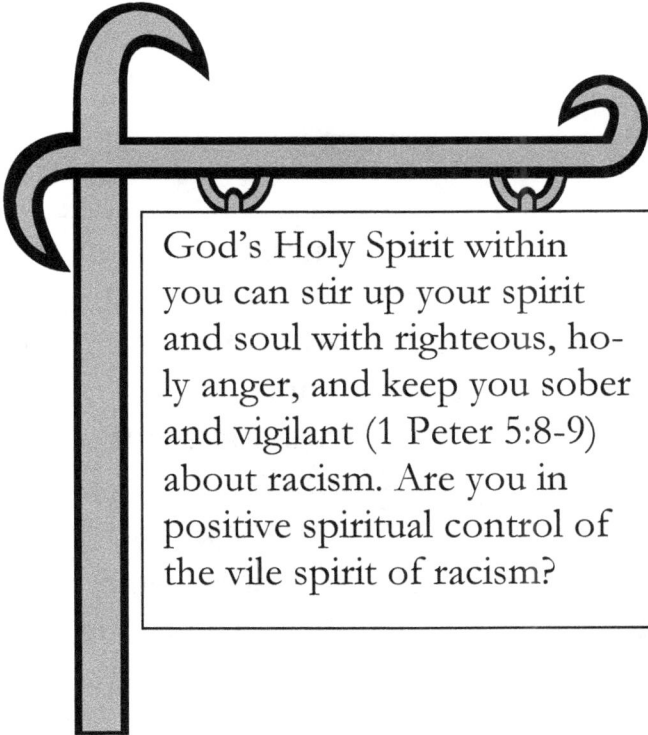

God's Holy Spirit within you can stir up your spirit and soul with righteous, holy anger, and keep you sober and vigilant (1 Peter 5:8-9) about racism. Are you in positive spiritual control of the vile spirit of racism?

9

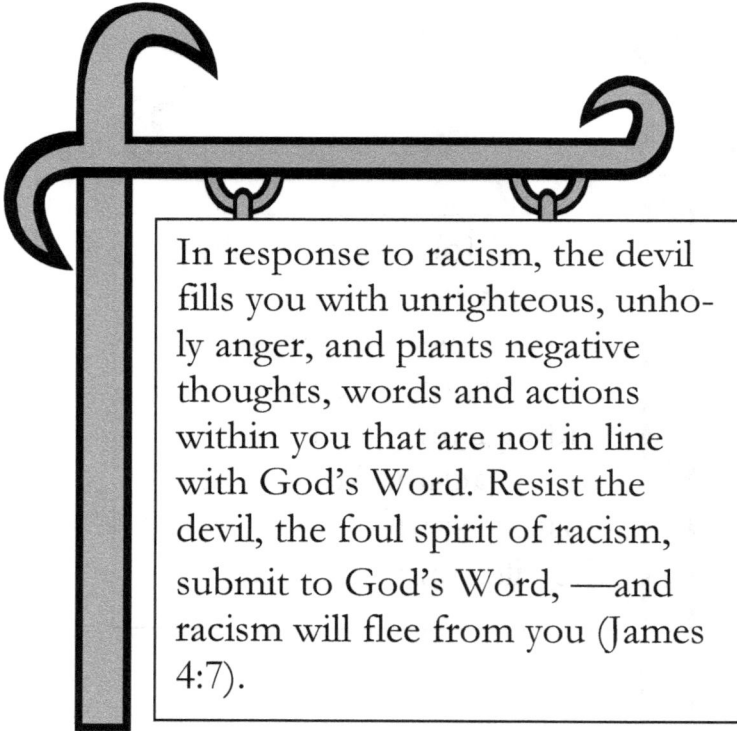

In response to racism, the devil fills you with unrighteous, unholy anger, and plants negative thoughts, words and actions within you that are not in line with God's Word. Resist the devil, the foul spirit of racism, submit to God's Word, —and racism will flee from you (James 4:7).

10

Righteous anger keeps you in line with God's Word to walk always on God's grounds of integrity (Ephesians 4:1)—to be obedient to His Word and the just law of the state as you face racism. Allow God to deliver His impartial justice to every injustice of racism.

11

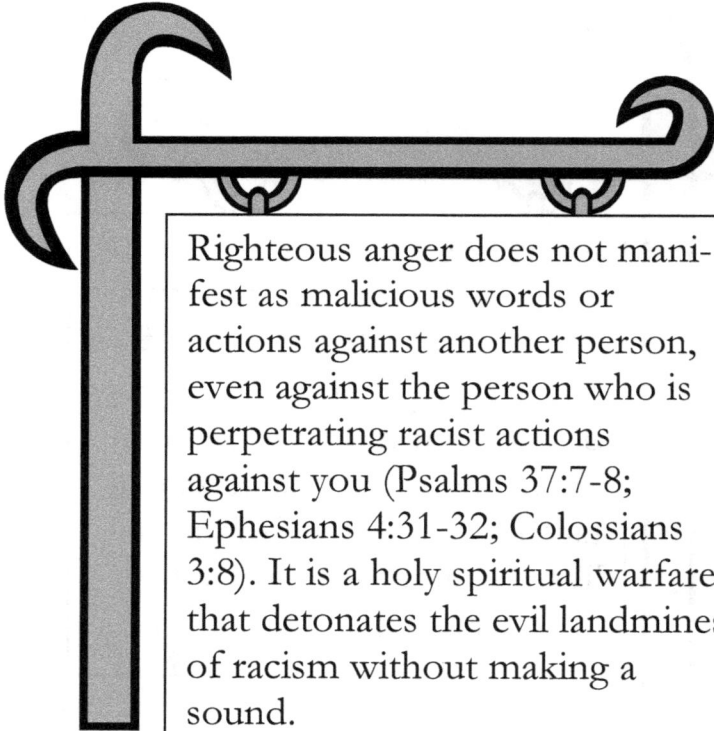

Righteous anger does not manifest as malicious words or actions against another person, even against the person who is perpetrating racist actions against you (Psalms 37:7-8; Ephesians 4:31-32; Colossians 3:8). It is a holy spiritual warfare that detonates the evil landmines of racism without making a sound.

12

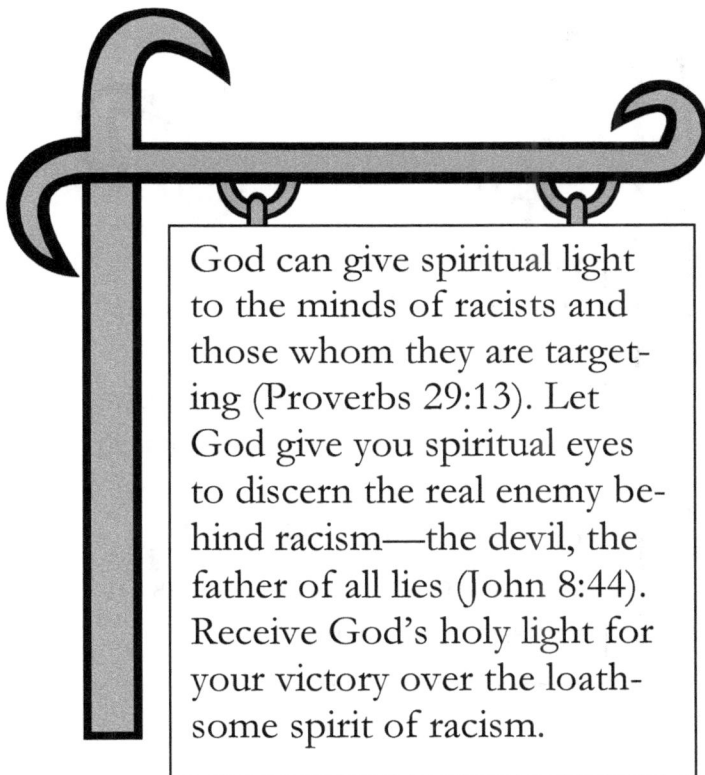

God can give spiritual light to the minds of racists and those whom they are targeting (Proverbs 29:13). Let God give you spiritual eyes to discern the real enemy behind racism—the devil, the father of all lies (John 8:44). Receive God's holy light for your victory over the loathsome spirit of racism.

13

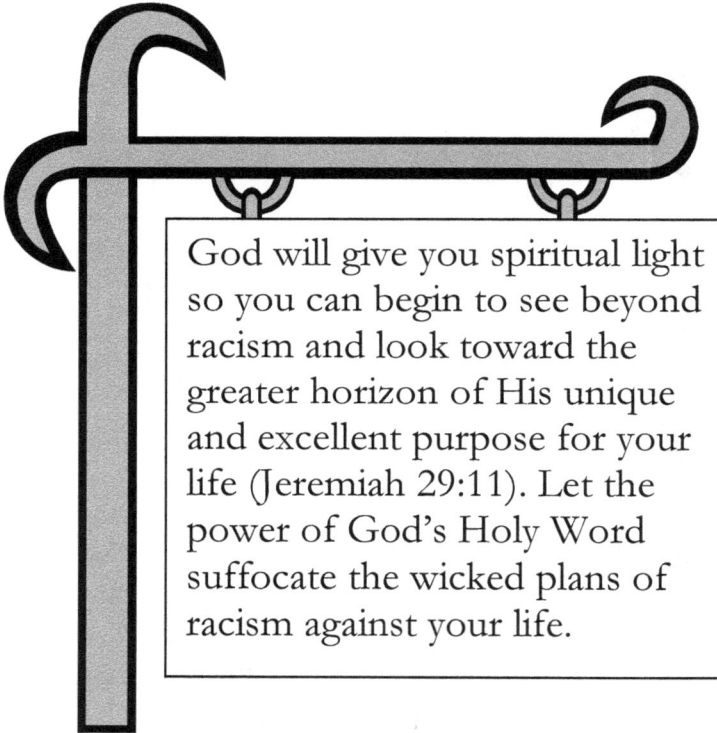

God will give you spiritual light so you can begin to see beyond racism and look toward the greater horizon of His unique and excellent purpose for your life (Jeremiah 29:11). Let the power of God's Holy Word suffocate the wicked plans of racism against your life.

14

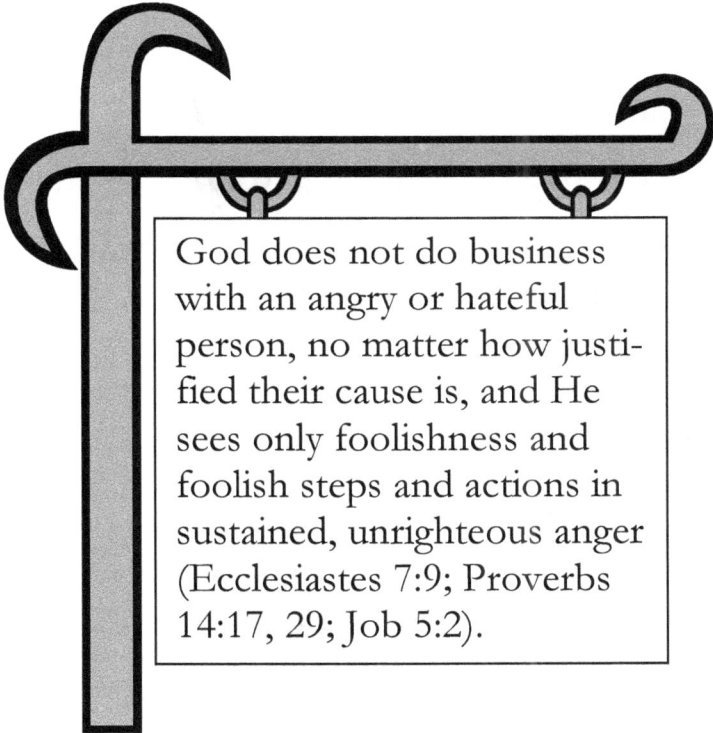

God does not do business with an angry or hateful person, no matter how justified their cause is, and He sees only foolishness and foolish steps and actions in sustained, unrighteous anger (Ecclesiastes 7:9; Proverbs 14:17, 29; Job 5:2).

15

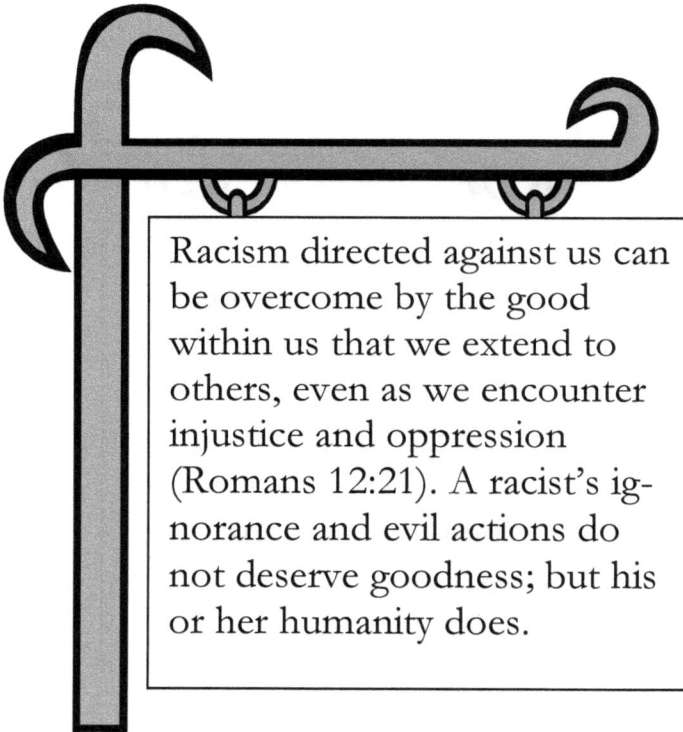

Racism directed against us can be overcome by the good within us that we extend to others, even as we encounter injustice and oppression (Romans 12:21). A racist's ignorance and evil actions do not deserve goodness; but his or her humanity does.

16

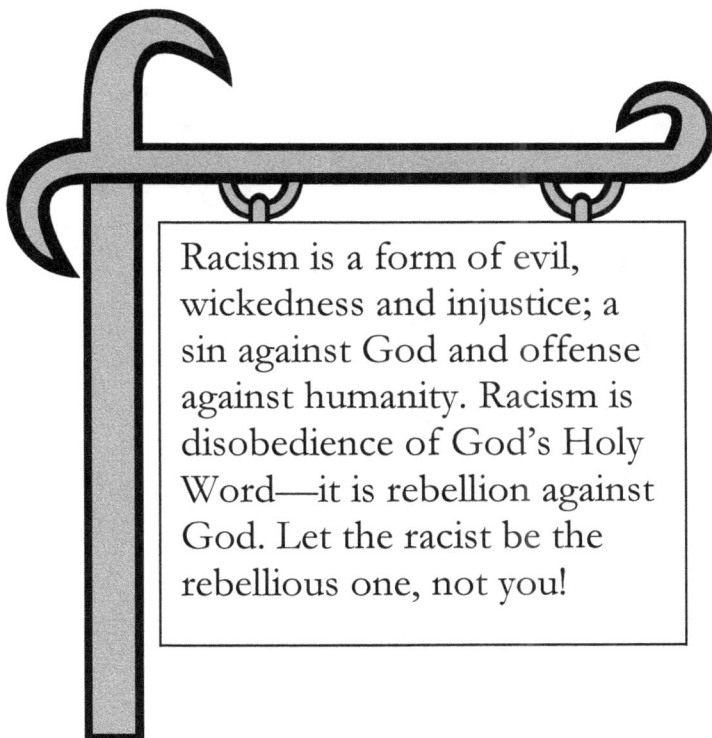

Racism is a form of evil, wickedness and injustice; a sin against God and offense against humanity. Racism is disobedience of God's Holy Word—it is rebellion against God. Let the racist be the rebellious one, not you!

17

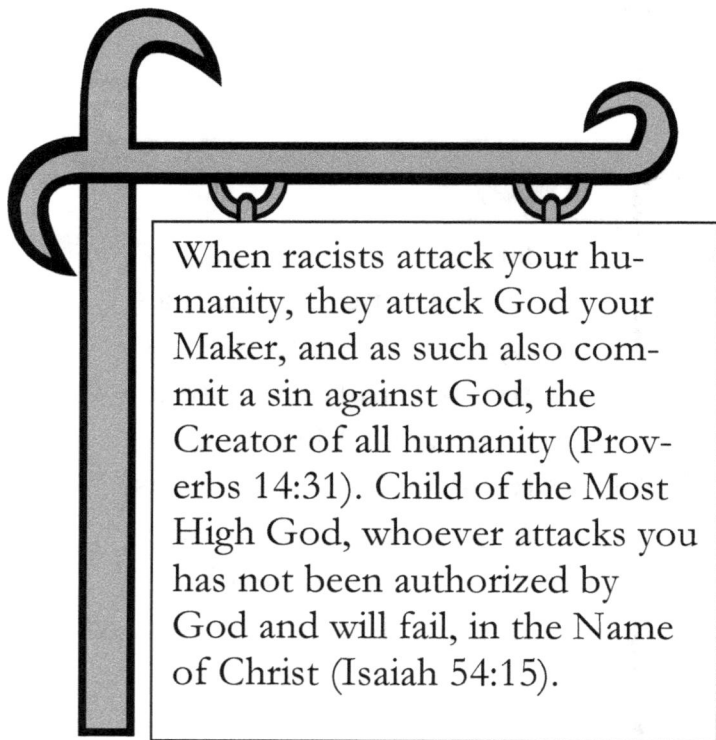

When racists attack your humanity, they attack God your Maker, and as such also commit a sin against God, the Creator of all humanity (Proverbs 14:31). Child of the Most High God, whoever attacks you has not been authorized by God and will fail, in the Name of Christ (Isaiah 54:15).

18

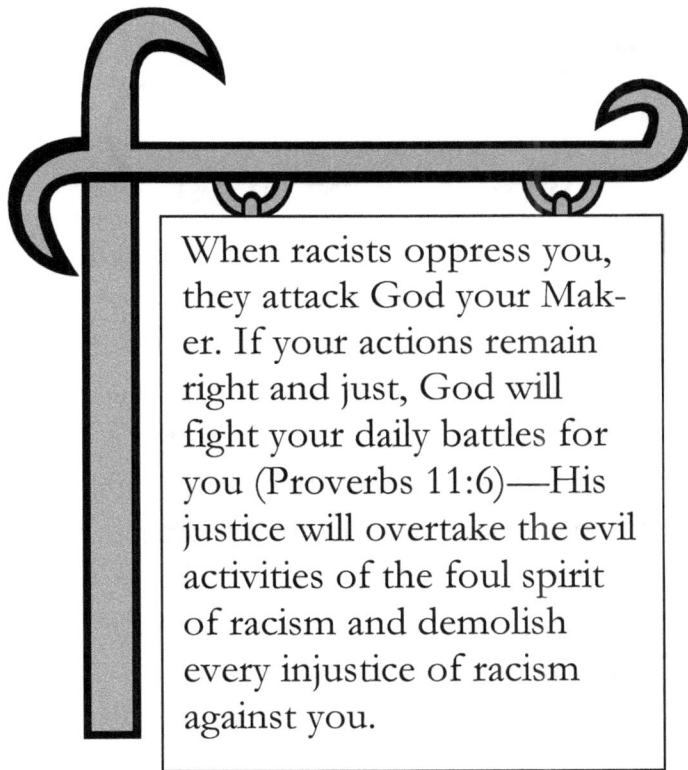

When racists oppress you, they attack God your Maker. If your actions remain right and just, God will fight your daily battles for you (Proverbs 11:6)—His justice will overtake the evil activities of the foul spirit of racism and demolish every injustice of racism against you.

19

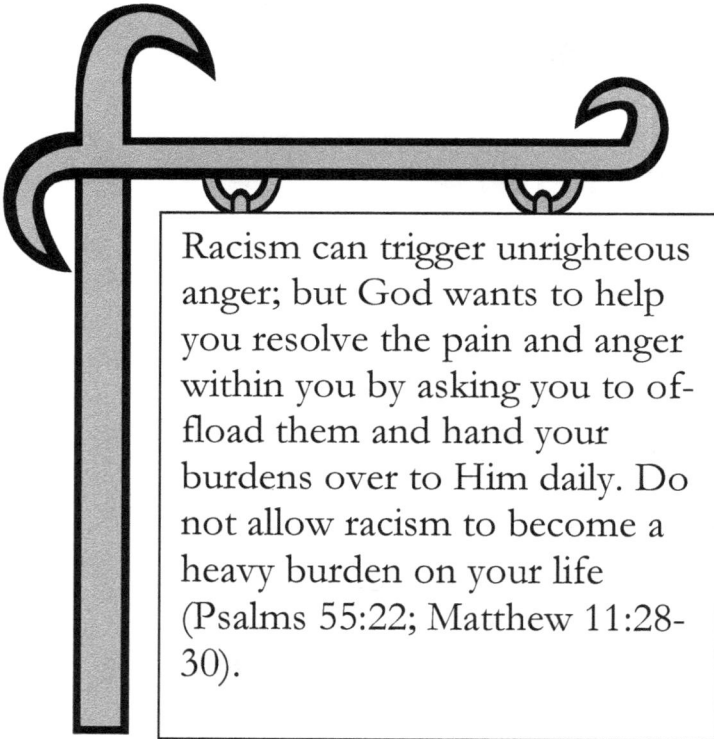

Racism can trigger unrighteous anger; but God wants to help you resolve the pain and anger within you by asking you to offload them and hand your burdens over to Him daily. Do not allow racism to become a heavy burden on your life (Psalms 55:22; Matthew 11:28-30).

20

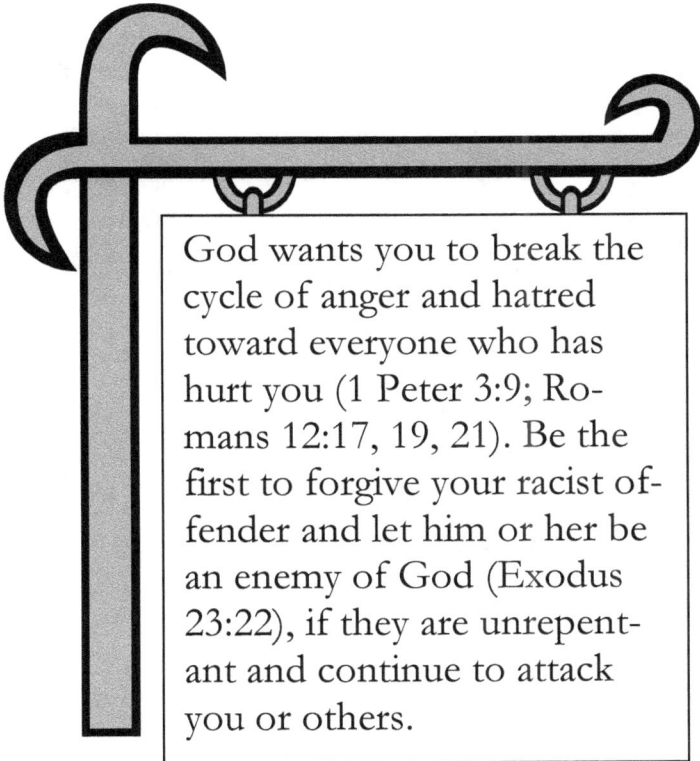

God wants you to break the cycle of anger and hatred toward everyone who has hurt you (1 Peter 3:9; Romans 12:17, 19, 21). Be the first to forgive your racist offender and let him or her be an enemy of God (Exodus 23:22), if they are unrepentant and continue to attack you or others.

21

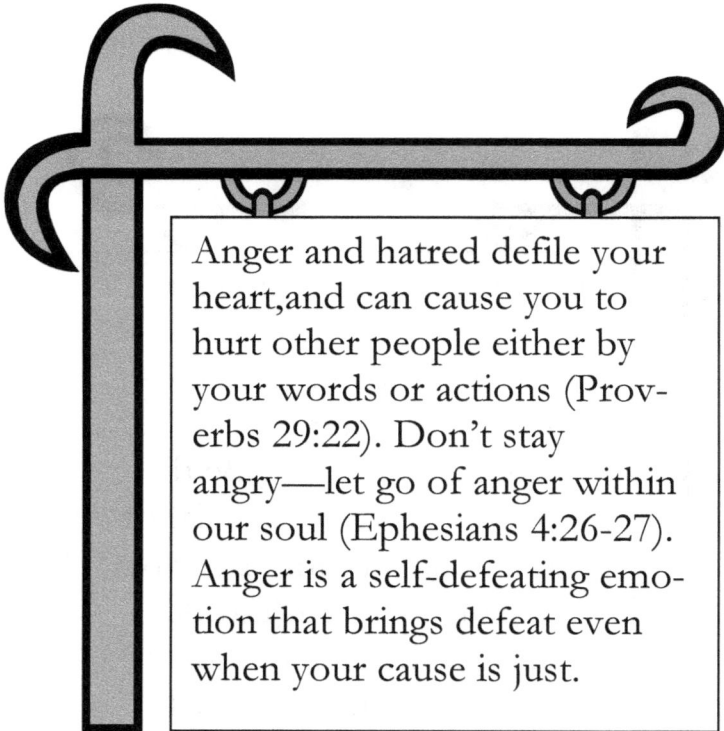

Anger and hatred defile your heart,and can cause you to hurt other people either by your words or actions (Proverbs 29:22). Don't stay angry—let go of anger within our soul (Ephesians 4:26-27). Anger is a self-defeating emotion that brings defeat even when your cause is just.

22

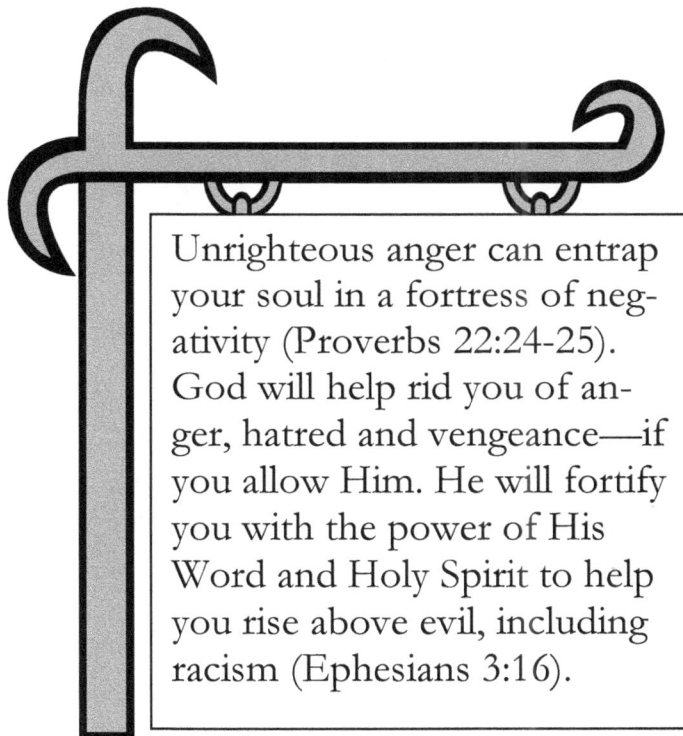

Unrighteous anger can entrap your soul in a fortress of negativity (Proverbs 22:24-25). God will help rid you of anger, hatred and vengeance—if you allow Him. He will fortify you with the power of His Word and Holy Spirit to help you rise above evil, including racism (Ephesians 3:16).

23

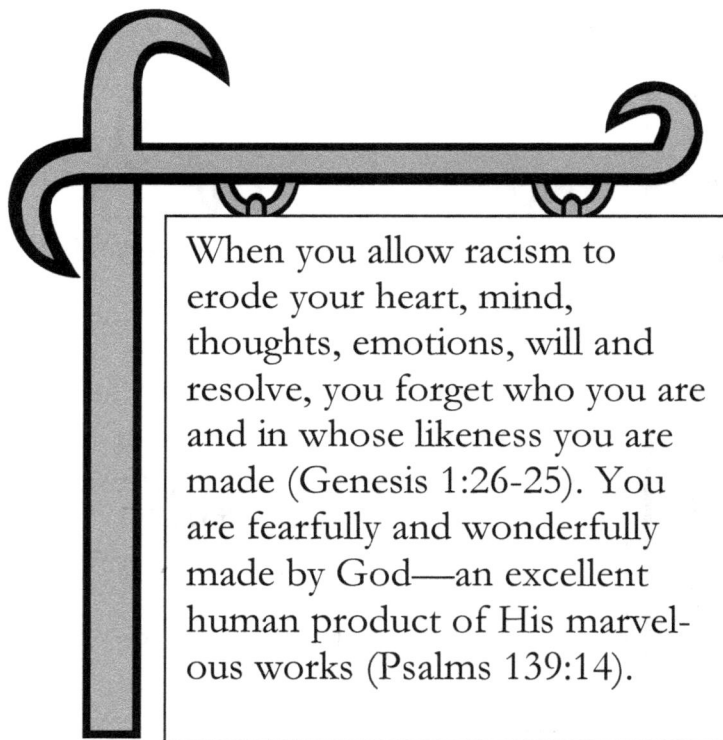

When you allow racism to erode your heart, mind, thoughts, emotions, will and resolve, you forget who you are and in whose likeness you are made (Genesis 1:26-25). You are fearfully and wonderfully made by God—an excellent human product of His marvelous works (Psalms 139:14).

24

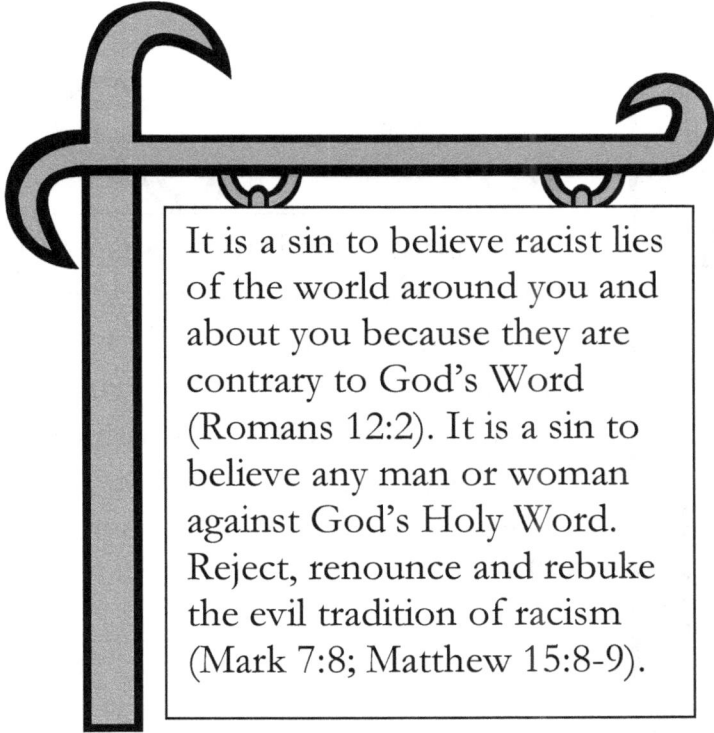

It is a sin to believe racist lies of the world around you and about you because they are contrary to God's Word (Romans 12:2). It is a sin to believe any man or woman against God's Holy Word. Reject, renounce and rebuke the evil tradition of racism (Mark 7:8; Matthew 15:8-9).

25

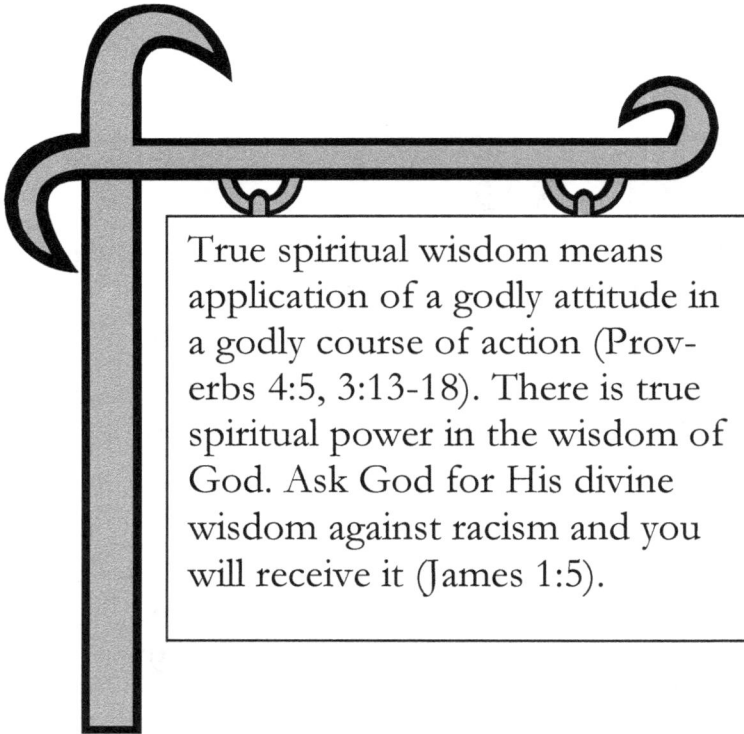

True spiritual wisdom means application of a godly attitude in a godly course of action (Proverbs 4:5, 3:13-18). There is true spiritual power in the wisdom of God. Ask God for His divine wisdom against racism and you will receive it (James 1:5).

26

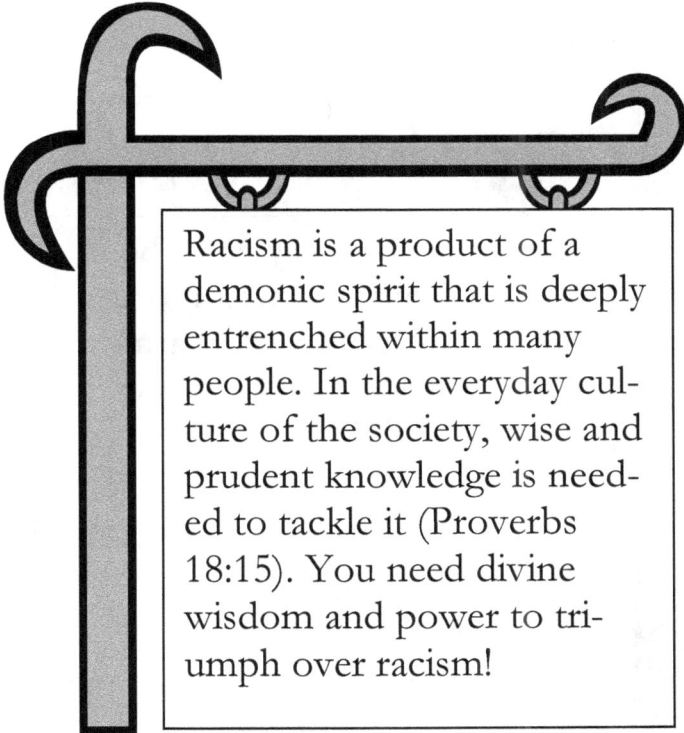

Racism is a product of a demonic spirit that is deeply entrenched within many people. In the everyday culture of the society, wise and prudent knowledge is needed to tackle it (Proverbs 18:15). You need divine wisdom and power to triumph over racism!

27

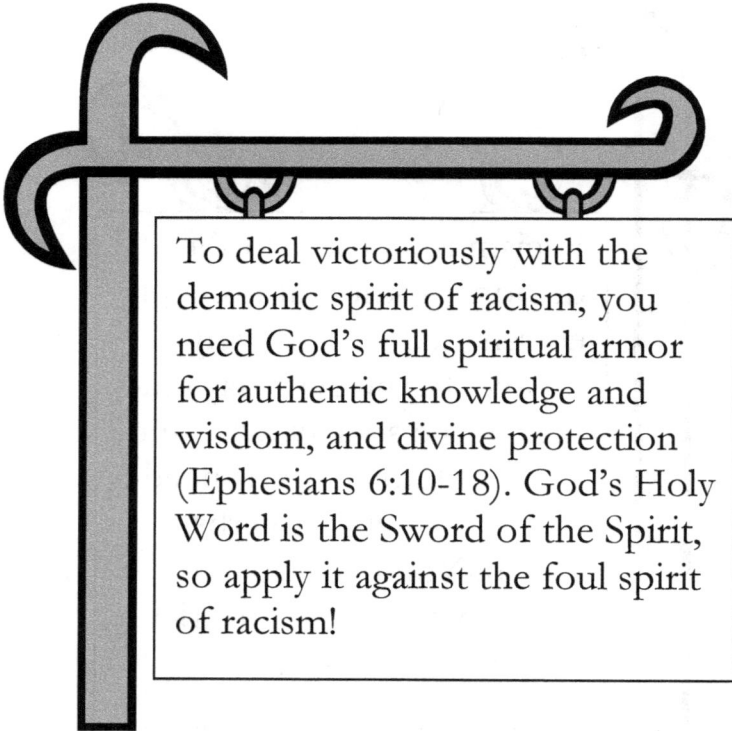

To deal victoriously with the demonic spirit of racism, you need God's full spiritual armor for authentic knowledge and wisdom, and divine protection (Ephesians 6:10-18). God's Holy Word is the Sword of the Spirit, so apply it against the foul spirit of racism!

28

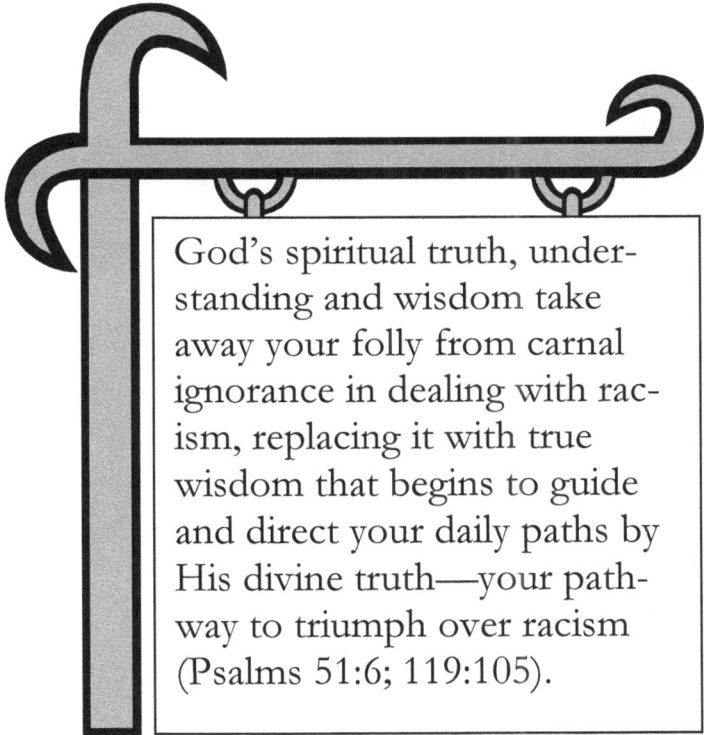

God's spiritual truth, understanding and wisdom take away your folly from carnal ignorance in dealing with racism, replacing it with true wisdom that begins to guide and direct your daily paths by His divine truth—your pathway to triumph over racism (Psalms 51:6; 119:105).

29

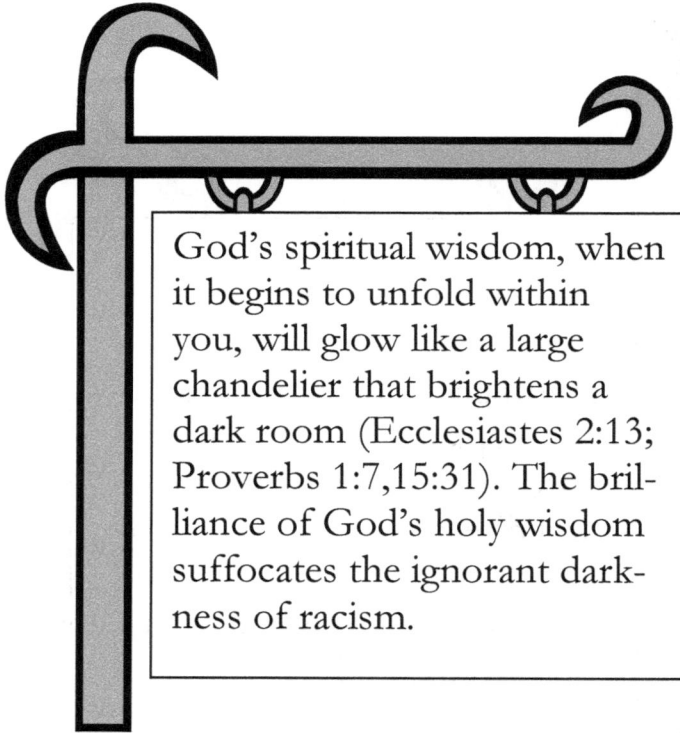

God's spiritual wisdom, when it begins to unfold within you, will glow like a large chandelier that brightens a dark room (Ecclesiastes 2:13; Proverbs 1:7,15:31). The brilliance of God's holy wisdom suffocates the ignorant darkness of racism.

30

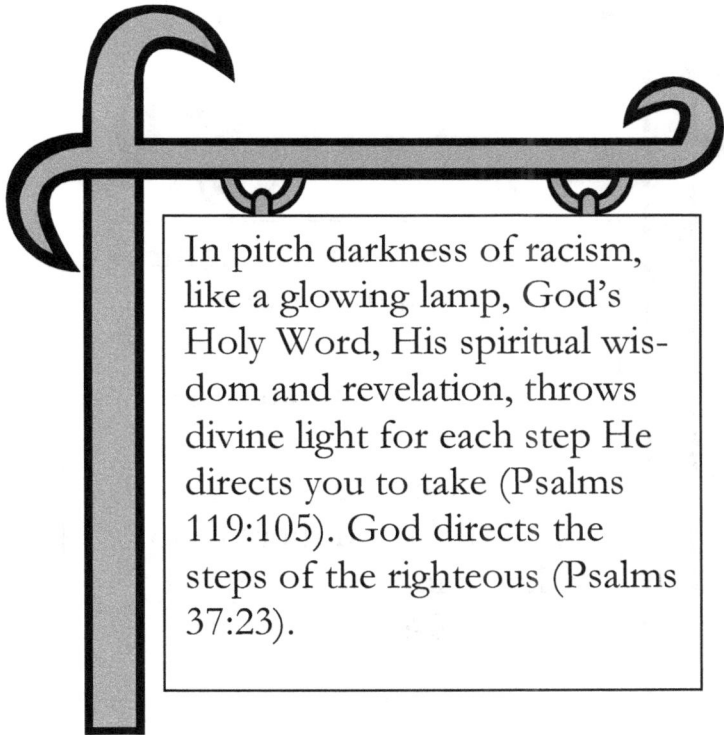

In pitch darkness of racism, like a glowing lamp, God's Holy Word, His spiritual wisdom and revelation, throws divine light for each step He directs you to take (Psalms 119:105). God directs the steps of the righteous (Psalms 37:23).

31

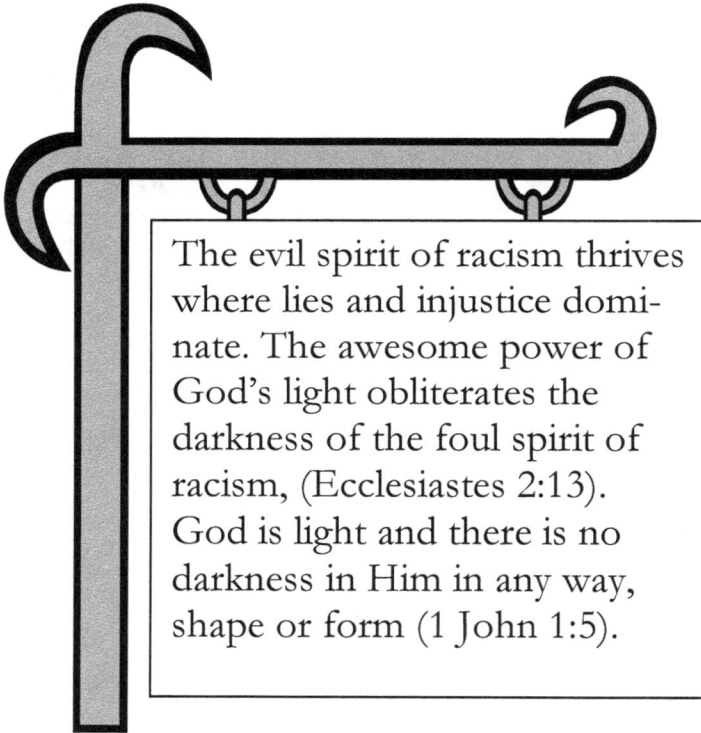

The evil spirit of racism thrives where lies and injustice dominate. The awesome power of God's light obliterates the darkness of the foul spirit of racism, (Ecclesiastes 2:13). God is light and there is no darkness in Him in any way, shape or form (1 John 1:5).

32

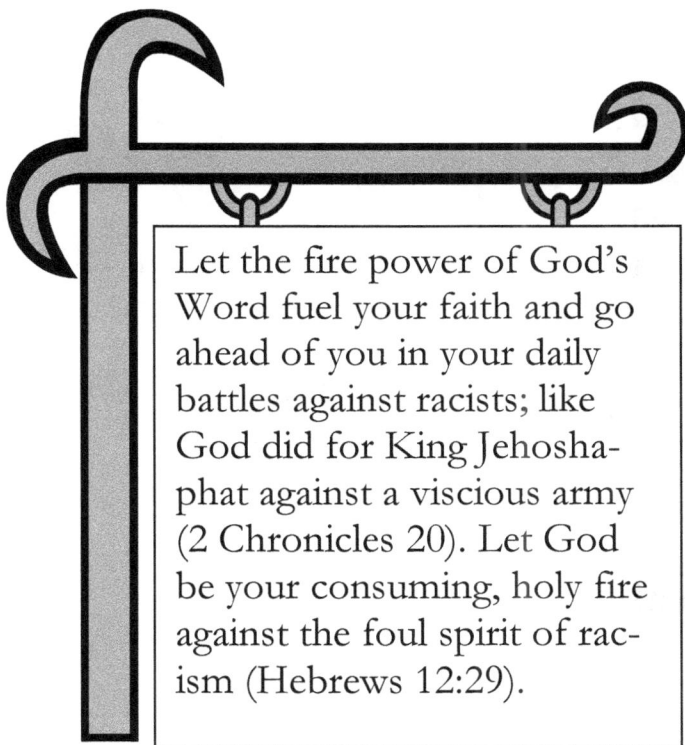

Let the fire power of God's Word fuel your faith and go ahead of you in your daily battles against racists; like God did for King Jehosha-phat against a viscious army (2 Chronicles 20). Let God be your consuming, holy fire against the foul spirit of rac-ism (Hebrews 12:29).

33

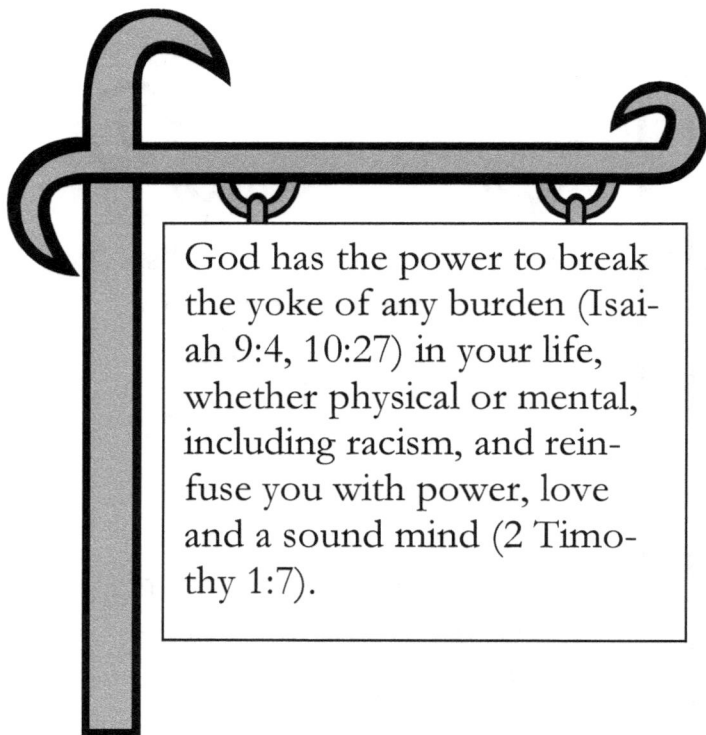

God has the power to break the yoke of any burden (Isaiah 9:4, 10:27) in your life, whether physical or mental, including racism, and reinfuse you with power, love and a sound mind (2 Timothy 1:7).

34

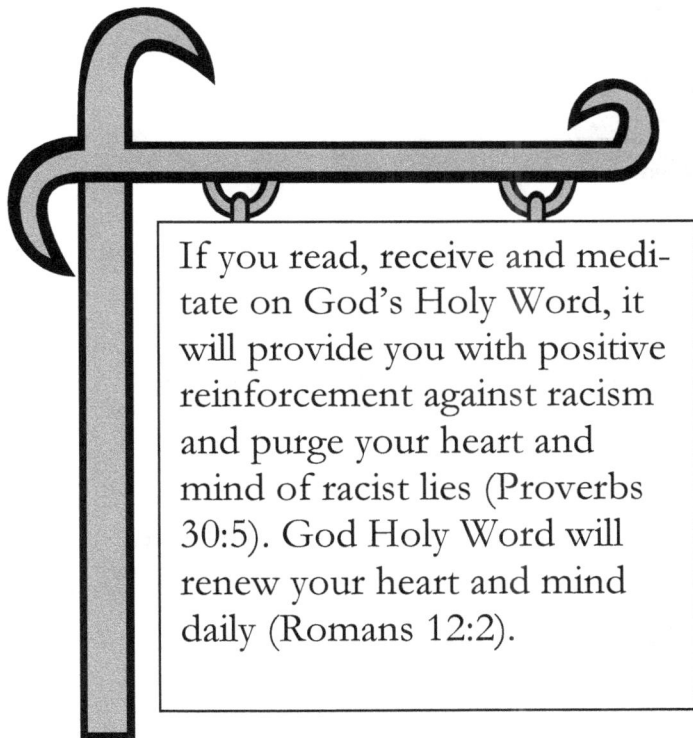

If you read, receive and meditate on God's Holy Word, it will provide you with positive reinforcement against racism and purge your heart and mind of racist lies (Proverbs 30:5). God Holy Word will renew your heart and mind daily (Romans 12:2).

35

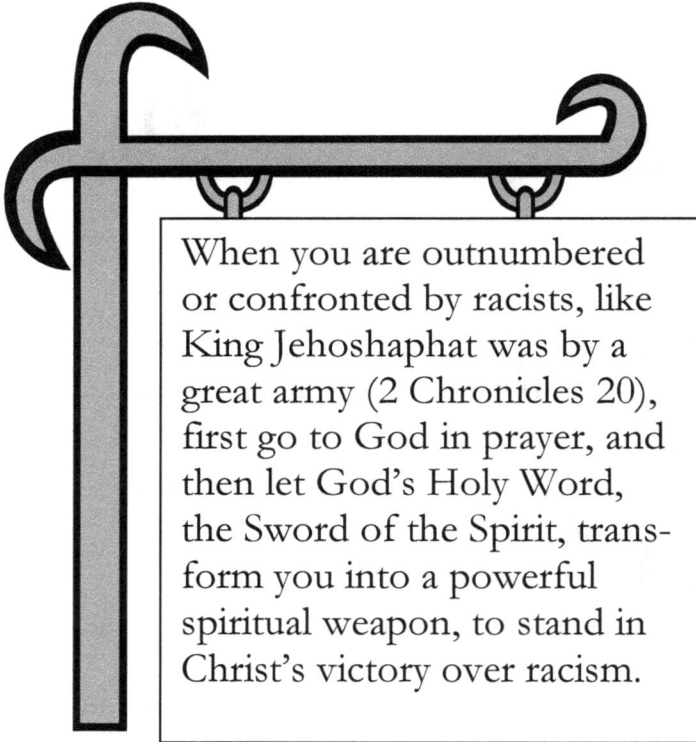

When you are outnumbered or confronted by racists, like King Jehoshaphat was by a great army (2 Chronicles 20), first go to God in prayer, and then let God's Holy Word, the Sword of the Spirit, transform you into a powerful spiritual weapon, to stand in Christ's victory over racism.

36

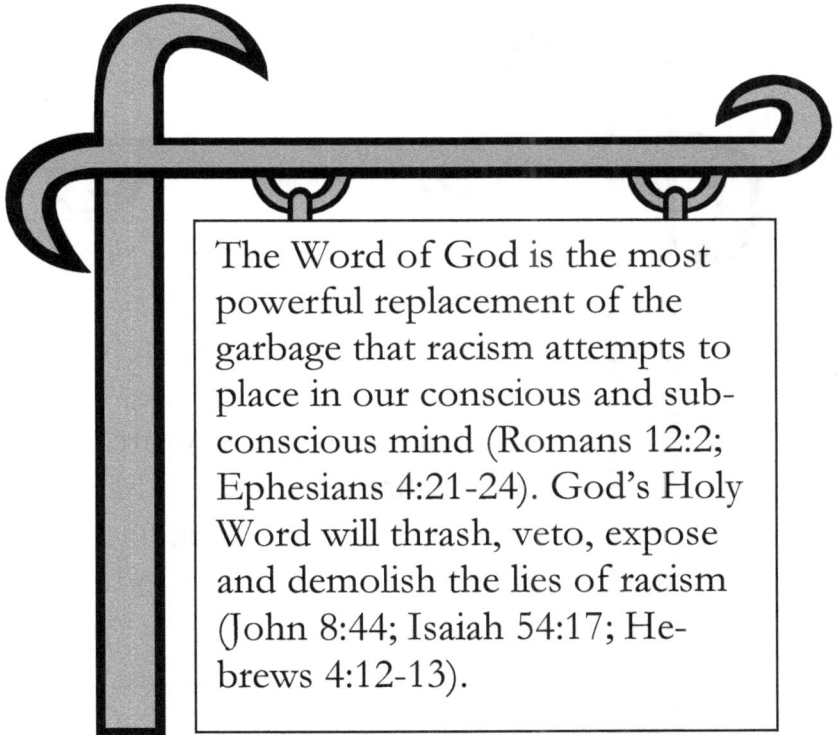

The Word of God is the most powerful replacement of the garbage that racism attempts to place in our conscious and subconscious mind (Romans 12:2; Ephesians 4:21-24). God's Holy Word will thrash, veto, expose and demolish the lies of racism (John 8:44; Isaiah 54:17; Hebrews 4:12-13).

37

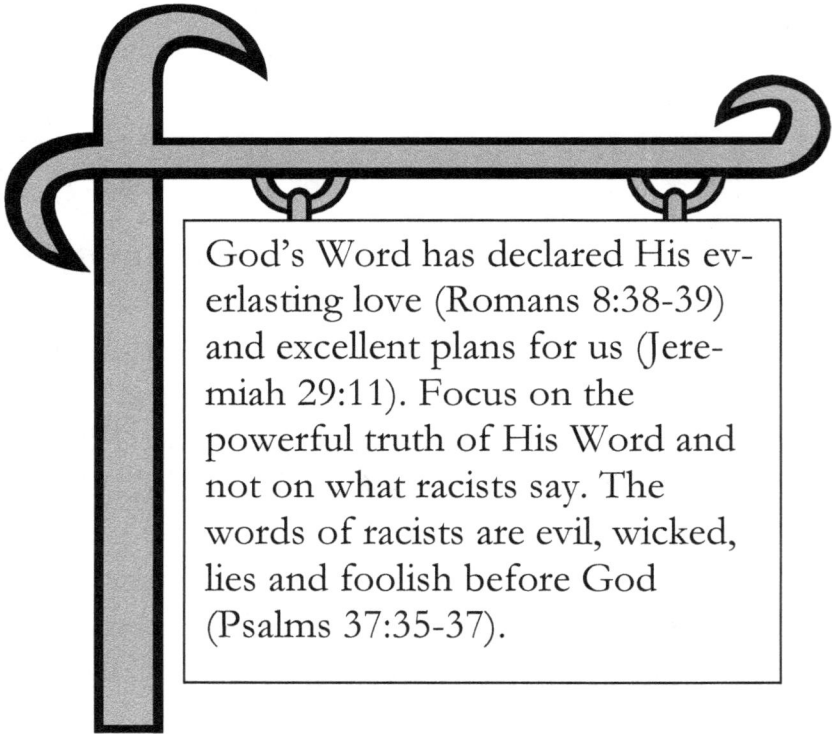

God's Word has declared His everlasting love (Romans 8:38-39) and excellent plans for us (Jeremiah 29:11). Focus on the powerful truth of His Word and not on what racists say. The words of racists are evil, wicked, lies and foolish before God (Psalms 37:35-37).

38

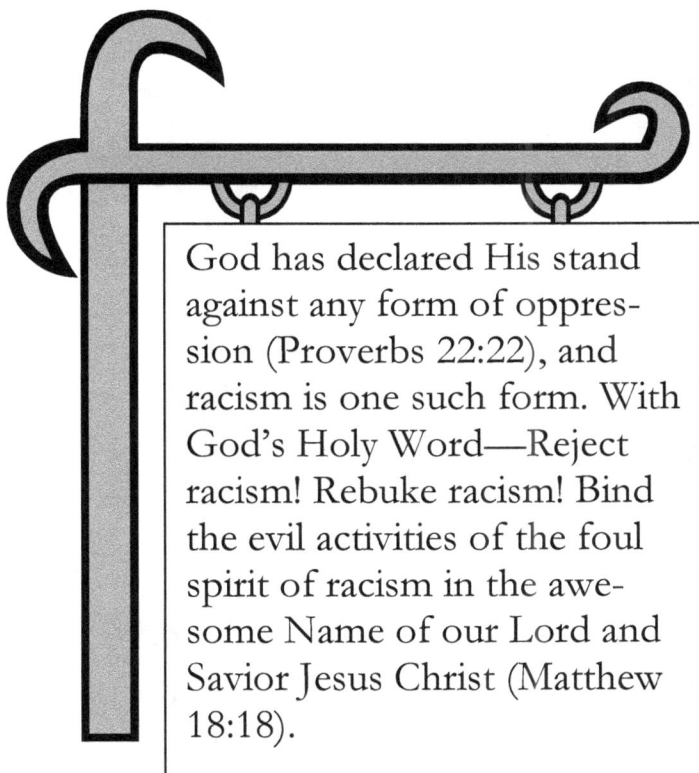

God has declared His stand against any form of oppression (Proverbs 22:22), and racism is one such form. With God's Holy Word—Reject racism! Rebuke racism! Bind the evil activities of the foul spirit of racism in the awesome Name of our Lord and Savior Jesus Christ (Matthew 18:18).

39

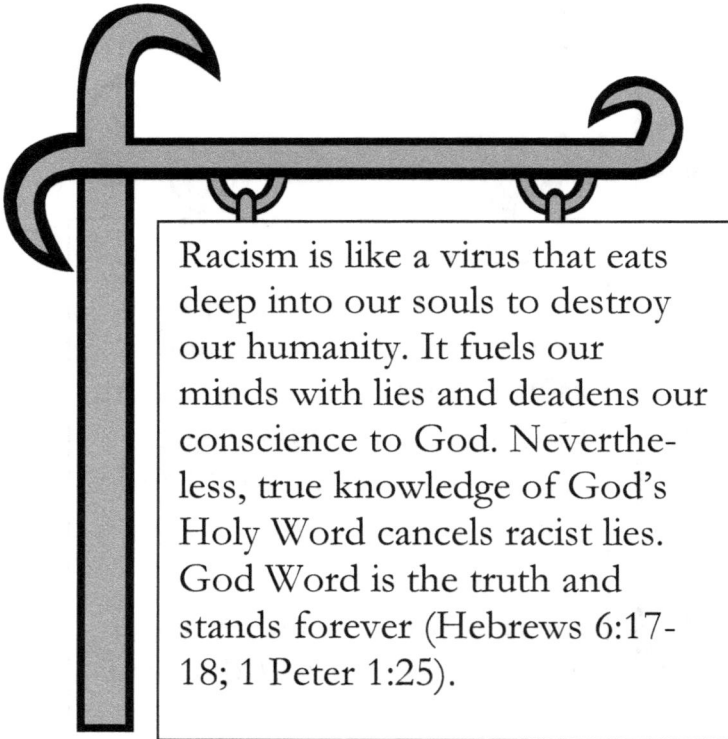

Racism is like a virus that eats deep into our souls to destroy our humanity. It fuels our minds with lies and deadens our conscience to God. Nevertheless, true knowledge of God's Holy Word cancels racist lies. God Word is the truth and stands forever (Hebrews 6:17-18; 1 Peter 1:25).

40

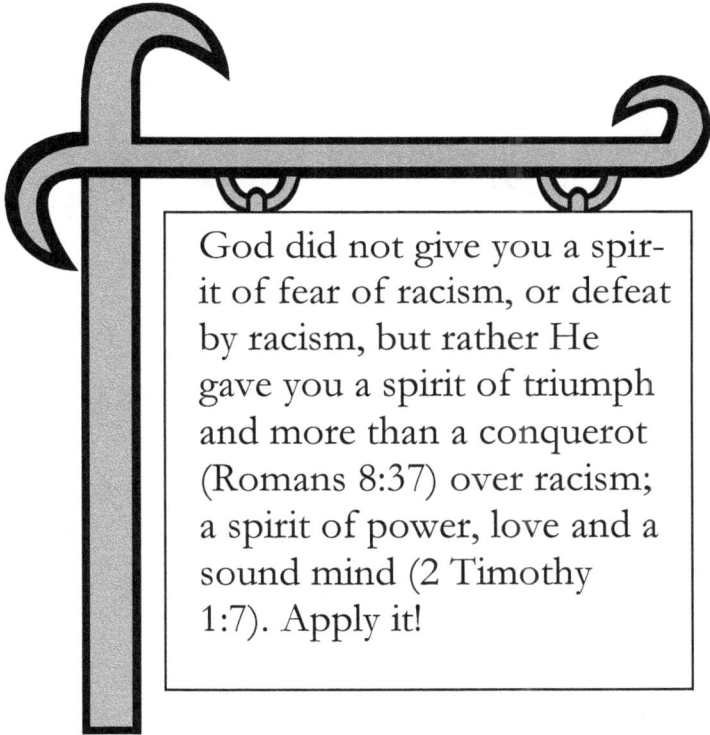

God did not give you a spirit of fear of racism, or defeat by racism, but rather He gave you a spirit of triumph and more than a conquerot (Romans 8:37) over racism; a spirit of power, love and a sound mind (2 Timothy 1:7). Apply it!

41

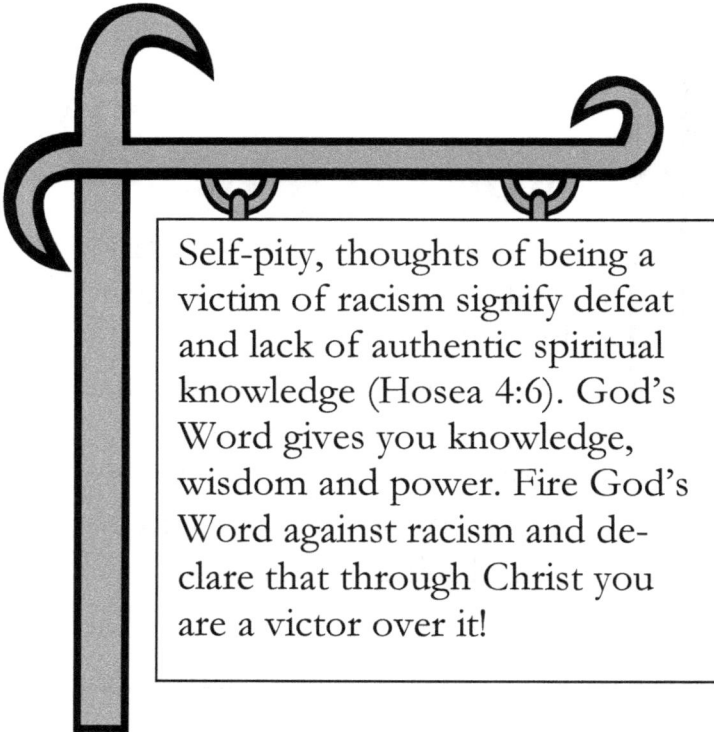

Self-pity, thoughts of being a victim of racism signify defeat and lack of authentic spiritual knowledge (Hosea 4:6). God's Word gives you knowledge, wisdom and power. Fire God's Word against racism and declare that through Christ you are a victor over it!

42

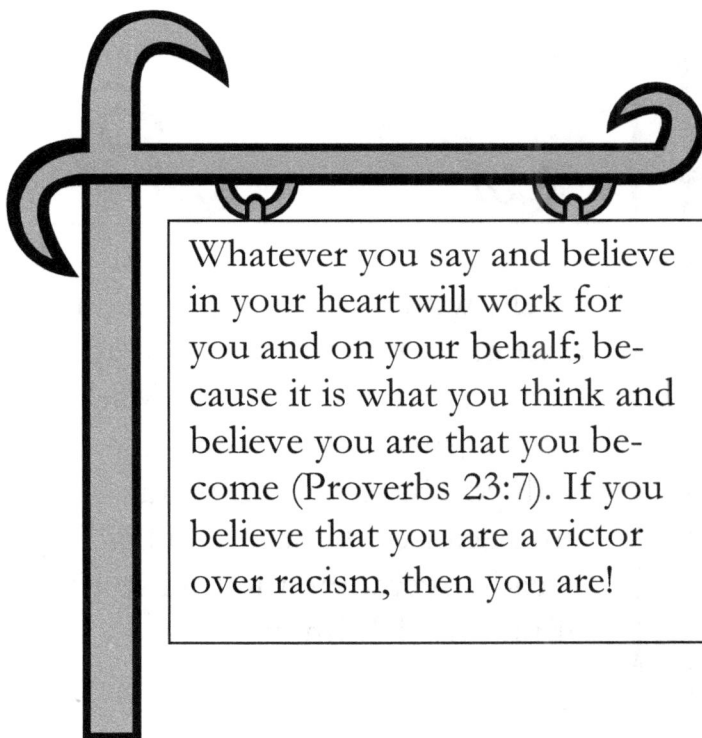

Whatever you say and believe in your heart will work for you and on your behalf; because it is what you think and believe you are that you become (Proverbs 23:7). If you believe that you are a victor over racism, then you are!

43

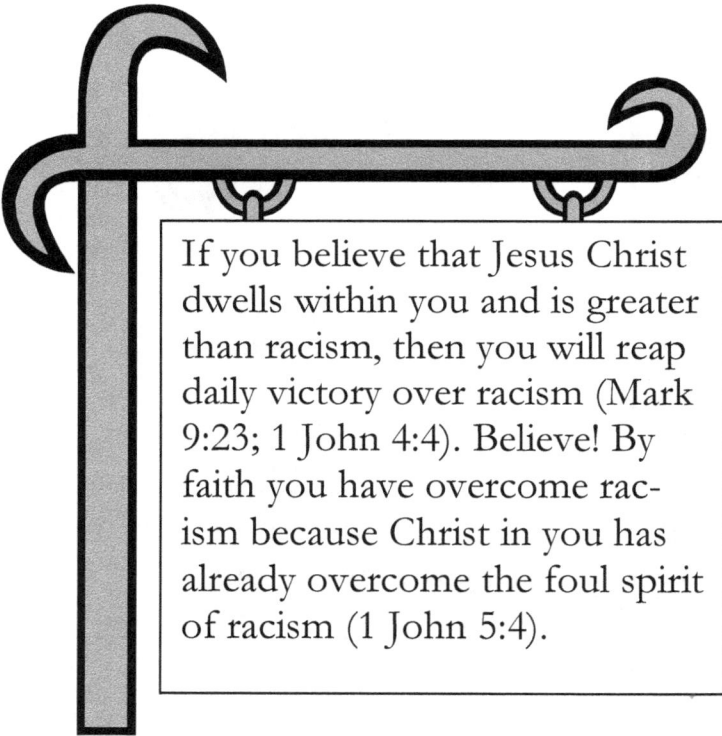

If you believe that Jesus Christ dwells within you and is greater than racism, then you will reap daily victory over racism (Mark 9:23; 1 John 4:4). Believe! By faith you have overcome racism because Christ in you has already overcome the foul spirit of racism (1 John 5:4).

44

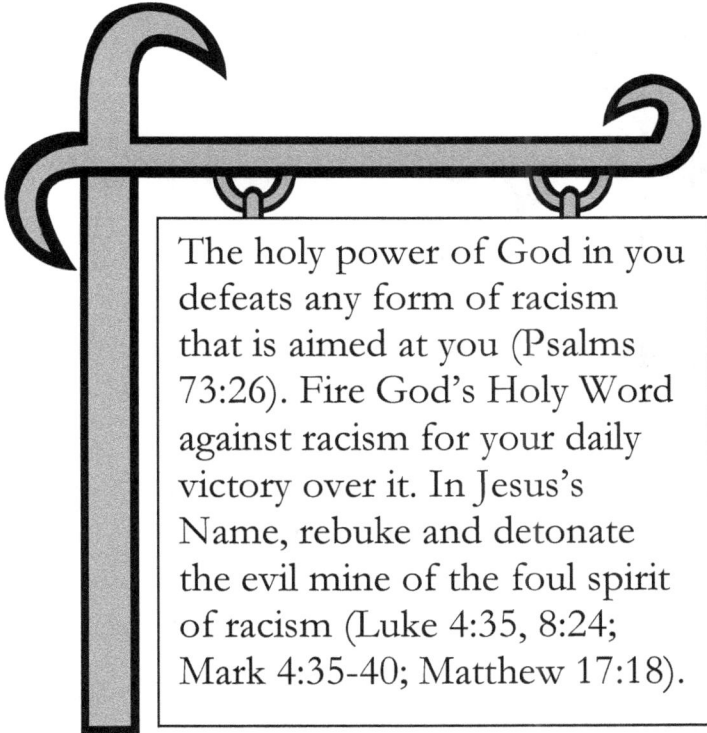

The holy power of God in you defeats any form of racism that is aimed at you (Psalms 73:26). Fire God's Holy Word against racism for your daily victory over it. In Jesus's Name, rebuke and detonate the evil mine of the foul spirit of racism (Luke 4:35, 8:24; Mark 4:35-40; Matthew 17:18).

45

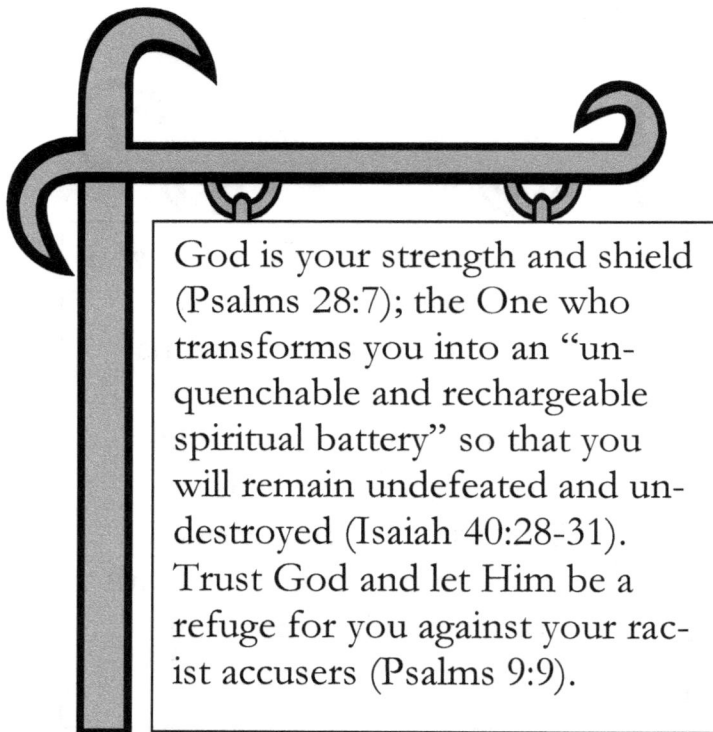

God is your strength and shield (Psalms 28:7); the One who transforms you into an "unquenchable and rechargeable spiritual battery" so that you will remain undefeated and undestroyed (Isaiah 40:28-31). Trust God and let Him be a refuge for you against your racist accusers (Psalms 9:9).

46

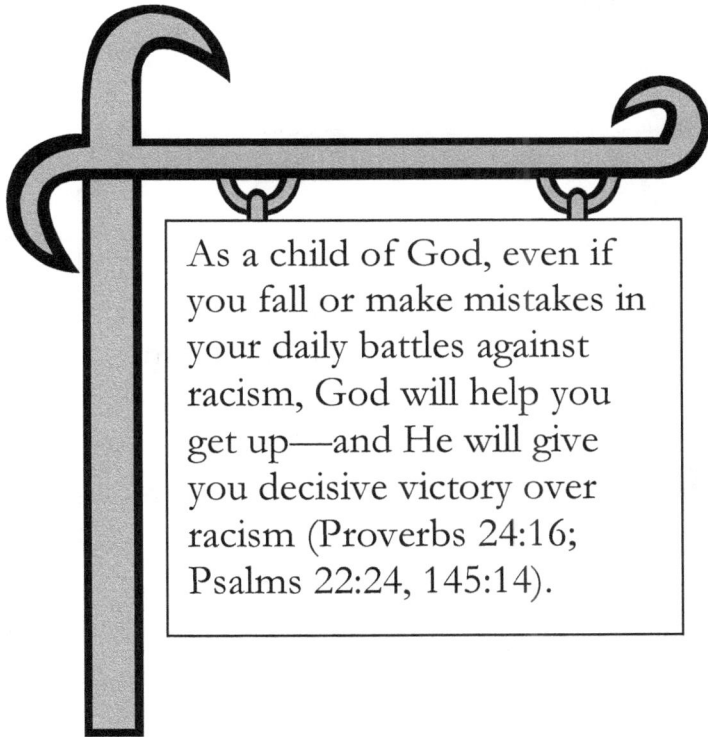

As a child of God, even if you fall or make mistakes in your daily battles against racism, God will help you get up—and He will give you decisive victory over racism (Proverbs 24:16; Psalms 22:24, 145:14).

47

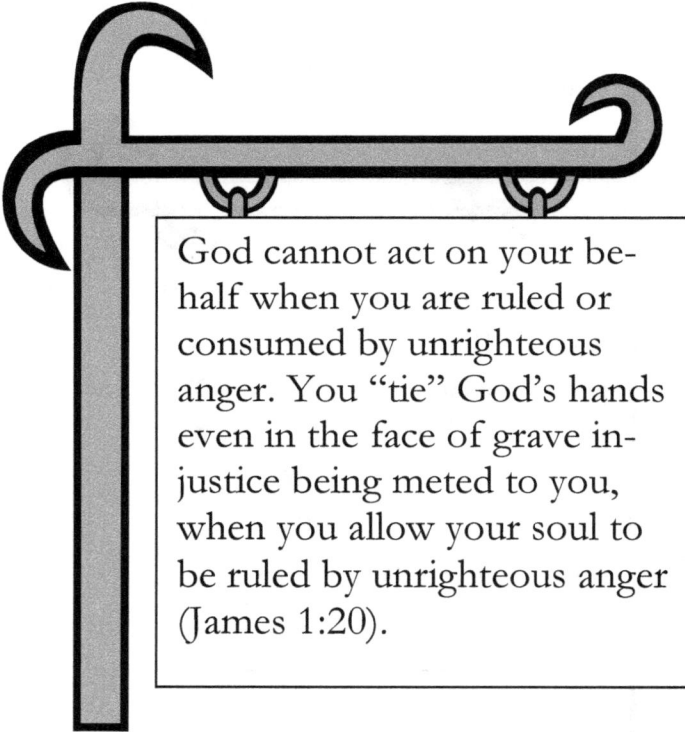

God cannot act on your behalf when you are ruled or
consumed by unrighteous
anger. You "tie" God's hands
even in the face of grave injustice being meted to you,
when you allow your soul to
be ruled by unrighteous anger
(James 1:20).

48

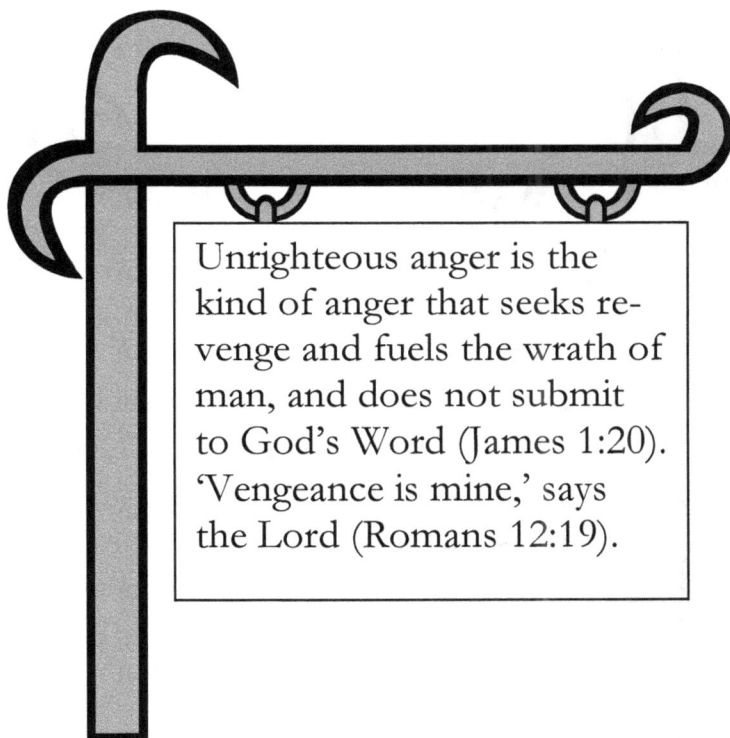

Unrighteous anger is the kind of anger that seeks revenge and fuels the wrath of man, and does not submit to God's Word (James 1:20). 'Vengeance is mine,' says the Lord (Romans 12:19).

49

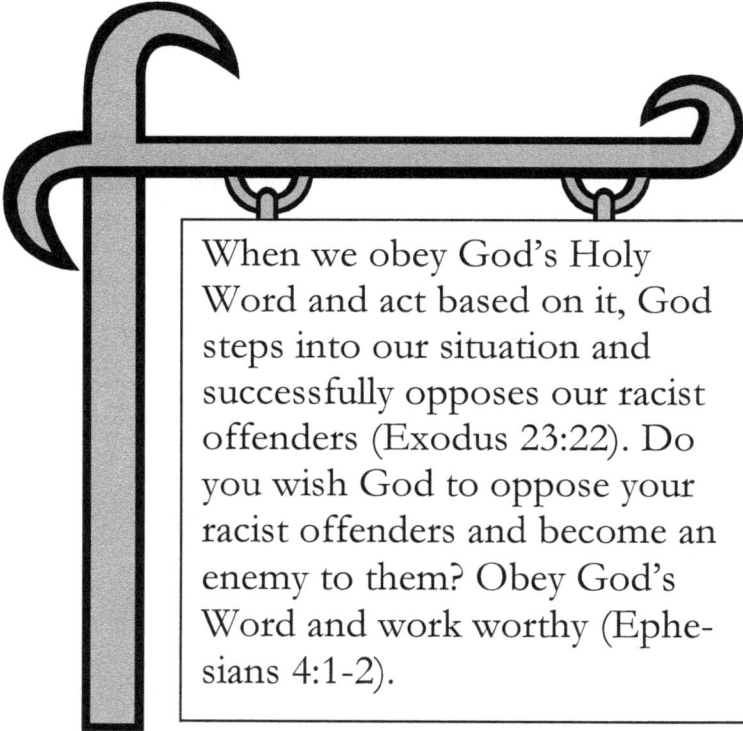

When we obey God's Holy Word and act based on it, God steps into our situation and successfully opposes our racist offenders (Exodus 23:22). Do you wish God to oppose your racist offenders and become an enemy to them? Obey God's Word and work worthy (Ephesians 4:1-2).

50

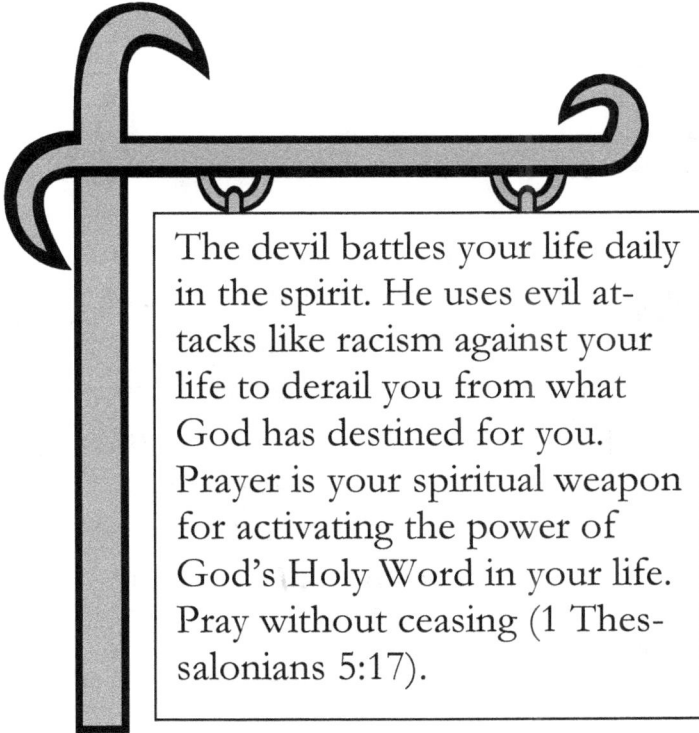

The devil battles your life daily in the spirit. He uses evil attacks like racism against your life to derail you from what God has destined for you. Prayer is your spiritual weapon for activating the power of God's Holy Word in your life. Pray without ceasing (1 Thessalonians 5:17).

51

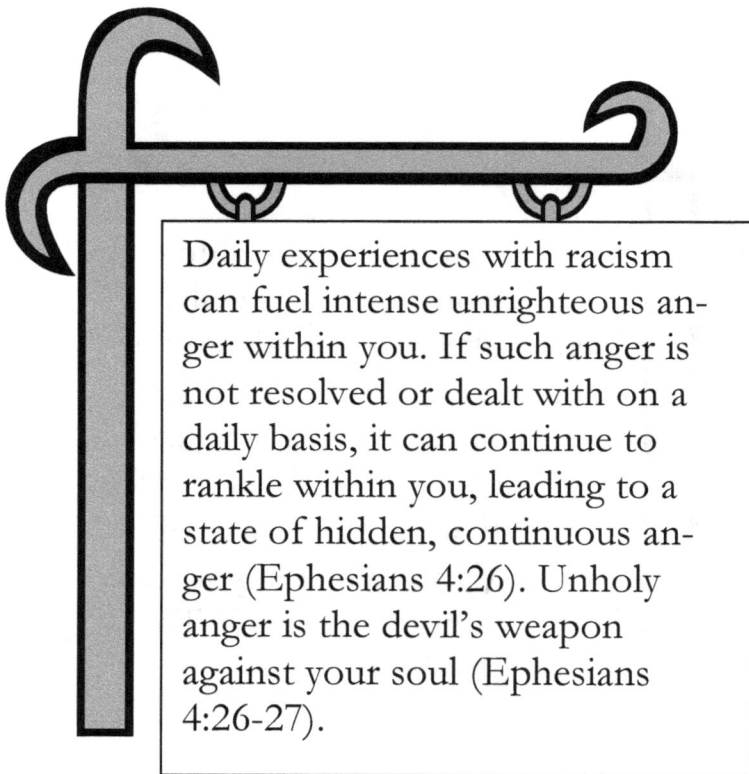

Daily experiences with racism can fuel intense unrighteous anger within you. If such anger is not resolved or dealt with on a daily basis, it can continue to rankle within you, leading to a state of hidden, continuous anger (Ephesians 4:26). Unholy anger is the devil's weapon against your soul (Ephesians 4:26-27).

52

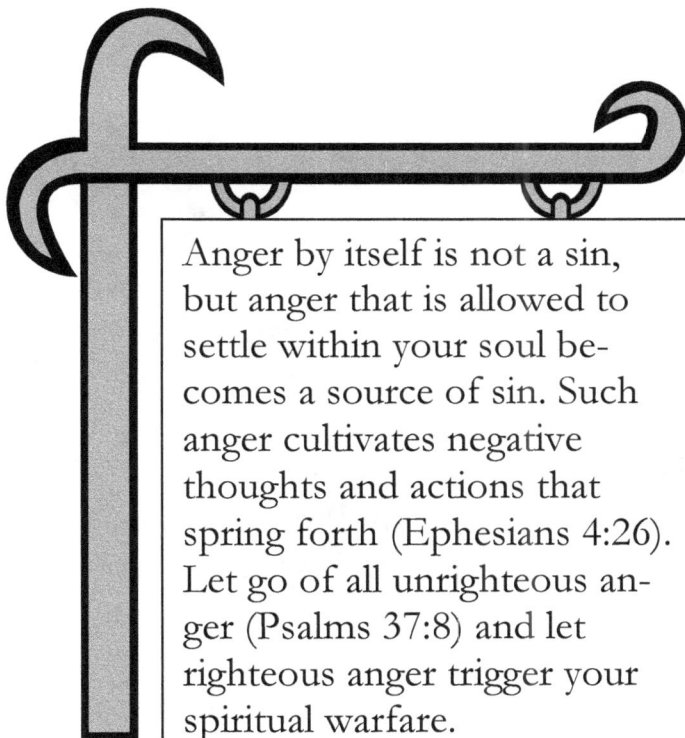

Anger by itself is not a sin, but anger that is allowed to settle within your soul becomes a source of sin. Such anger cultivates negative thoughts and actions that spring forth (Ephesians 4:26). Let go of all unrighteous anger (Psalms 37:8) and let righteous anger trigger your spiritual warfare.

53

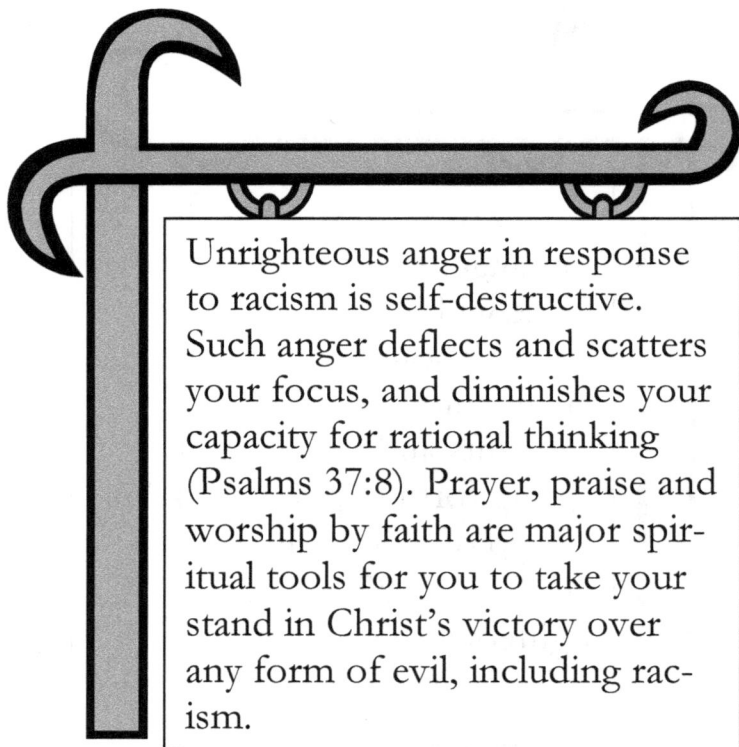

Unrighteous anger in response to racism is self-destructive. Such anger deflects and scatters your focus, and diminishes your capacity for rational thinking (Psalms 37:8). Prayer, praise and worship by faith are major spiritual tools for you to take your stand in Christ's victory over any form of evil, including racism.

54

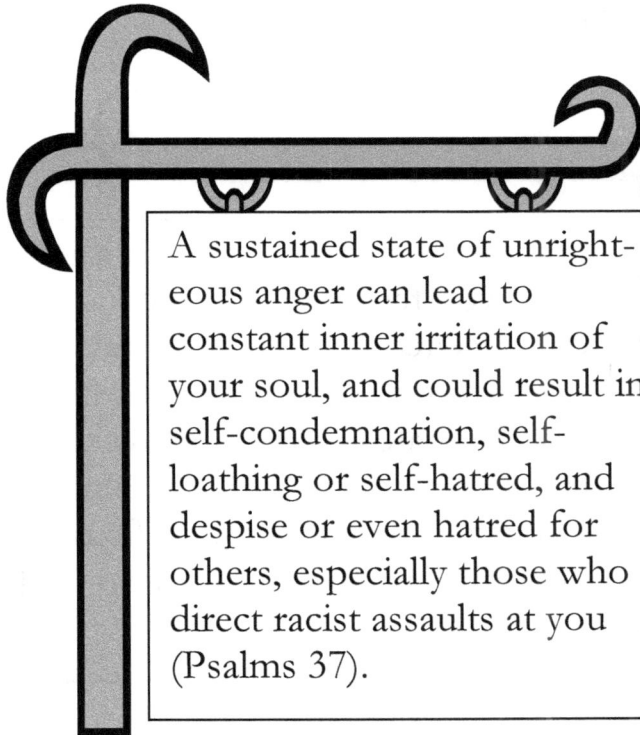

A sustained state of unrighteous anger can lead to
constant inner irritation of
your soul, and could result in
self-condemnation, self-
loathing or self-hatred, and
despise or even hatred for
others, especially those who
direct racist assaults at you
(Psalms 37).

55

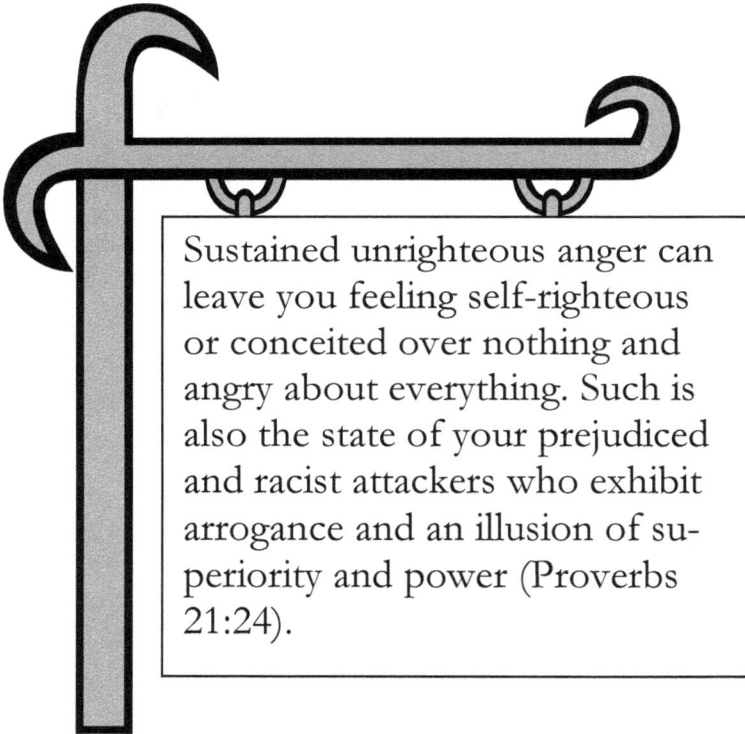

Sustained unrighteous anger can leave you feeling self-righteous or conceited over nothing and angry about everything. Such is also the state of your prejudiced and racist attackers who exhibit arrogance and an illusion of superiority and power (Proverbs 21:24).

56

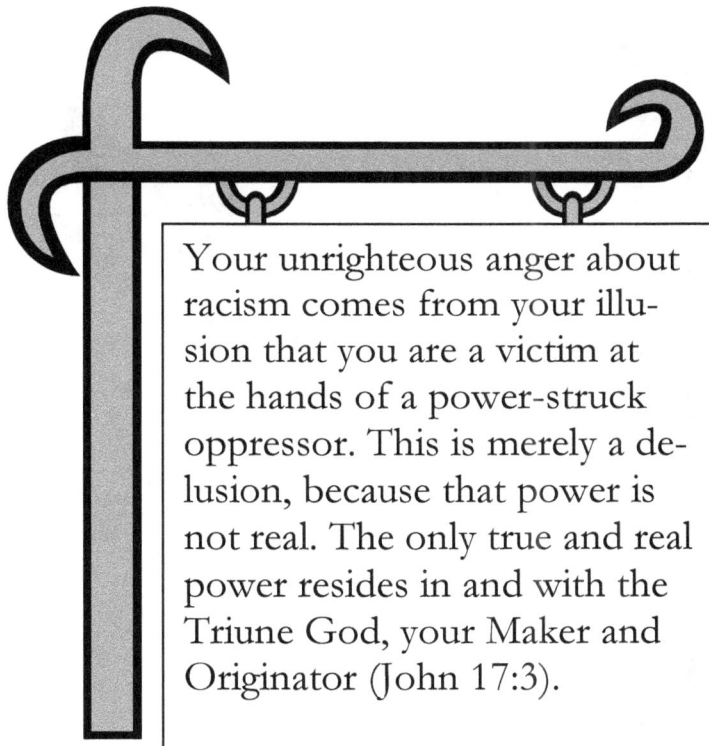

Your unrighteous anger about racism comes from your illusion that you are a victim at the hands of a power-struck oppressor. This is merely a delusion, because that power is not real. The only true and real power resides in and with the Triune God, your Maker and Originator (John 17:3).

57

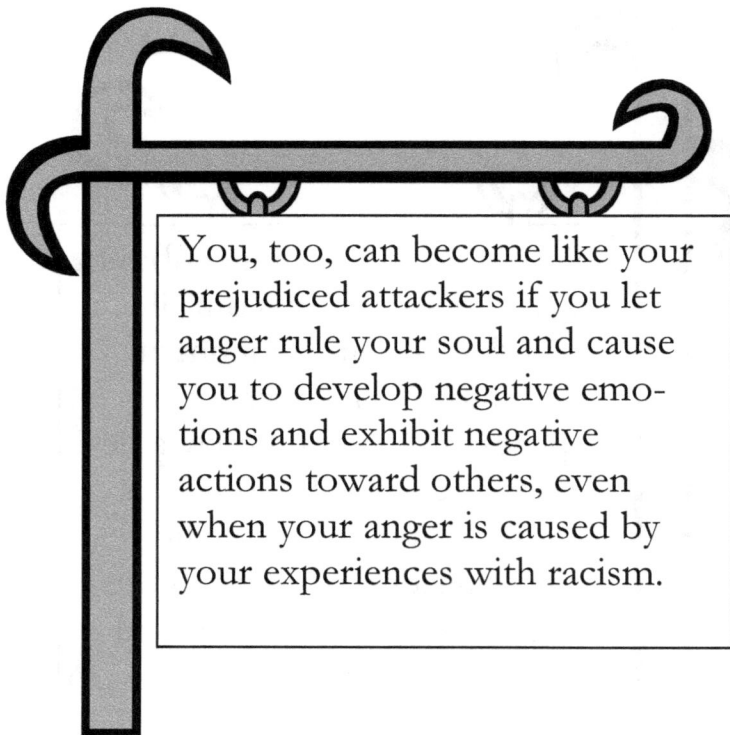

You, too, can become like your prejudiced attackers if you let anger rule your soul and cause you to develop negative emotions and exhibit negative actions toward others, even when your anger is caused by your experiences with racism.

58

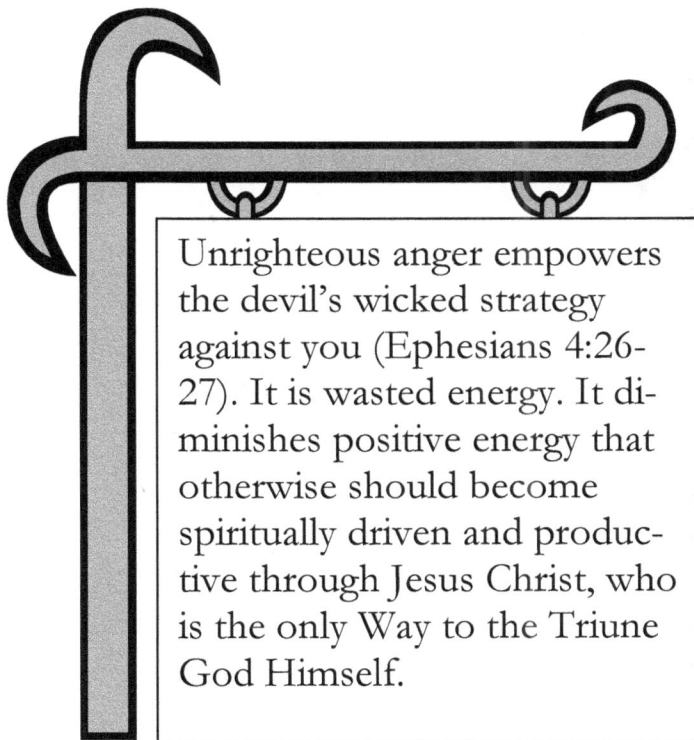

Unrighteous anger empowers the devil's wicked strategy against you (Ephesians 4:26-27). It is wasted energy. It diminishes positive energy that otherwise should become spiritually driven and productive through Jesus Christ, who is the only Way to the Triune God Himself.

59

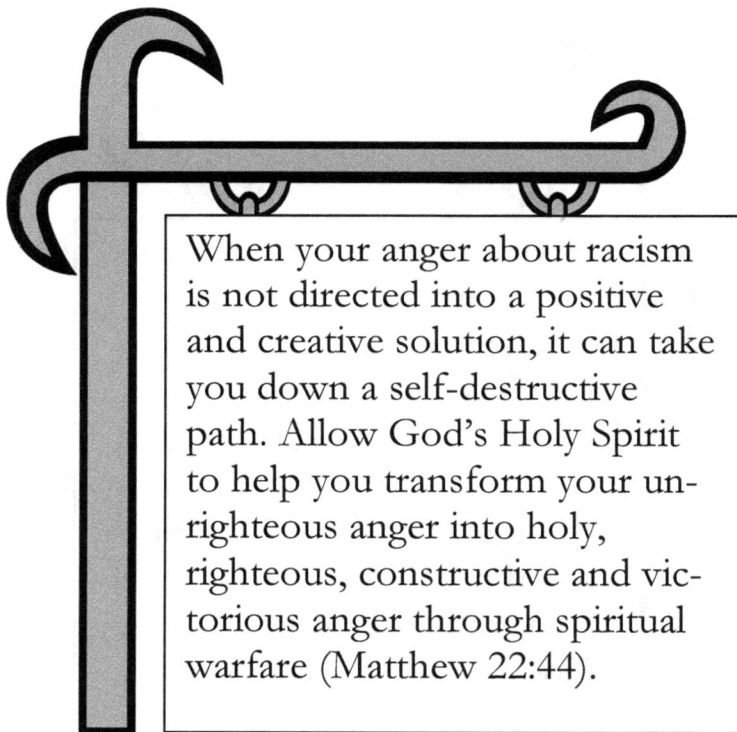

When your anger about racism is not directed into a positive and creative solution, it can take you down a self-destructive path. Allow God's Holy Spirit to help you transform your un-righteous anger into holy, righteous, constructive and victorious anger through spiritual warfare (Matthew 22:44).

60

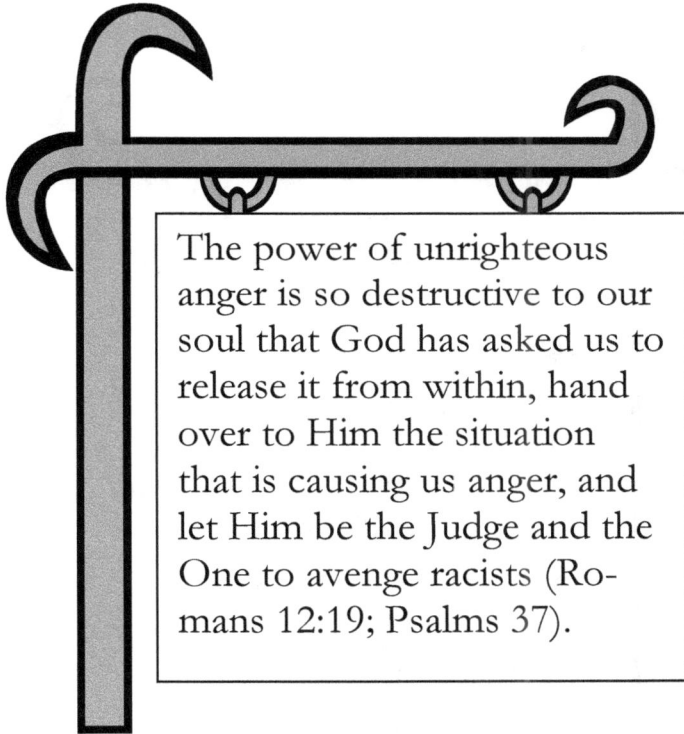

The power of unrighteous anger is so destructive to our soul that God has asked us to release it from within, hand over to Him the situation that is causing us anger, and let Him be the Judge and the One to avenge racists (Romans 12:19; Psalms 37).

61

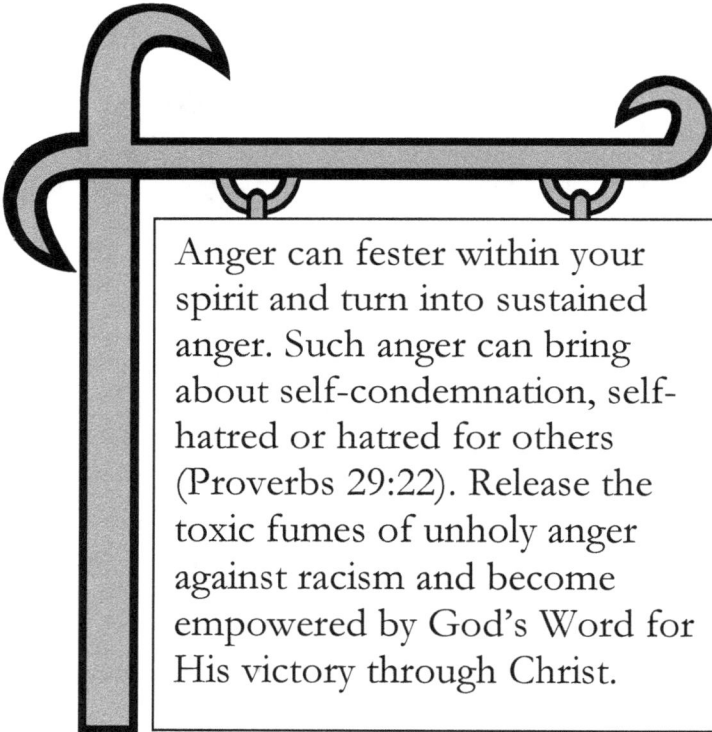

Anger can fester within your spirit and turn into sustained anger. Such anger can bring about self-condemnation, self-hatred or hatred for others (Proverbs 29:22). Release the toxic fumes of unholy anger against racism and become empowered by God's Word for His victory through Christ.

62

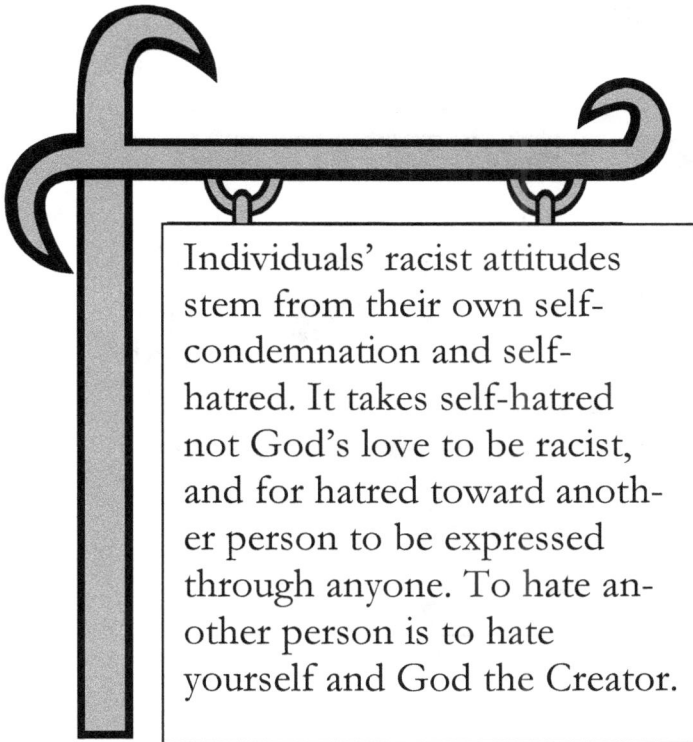

Individuals' racist attitudes stem from their own self-condemnation and self-hatred. It takes self-hatred not God's love to be racist, and for hatred toward another person to be expressed through anyone. To hate another person is to hate yourself and God the Creator.

63

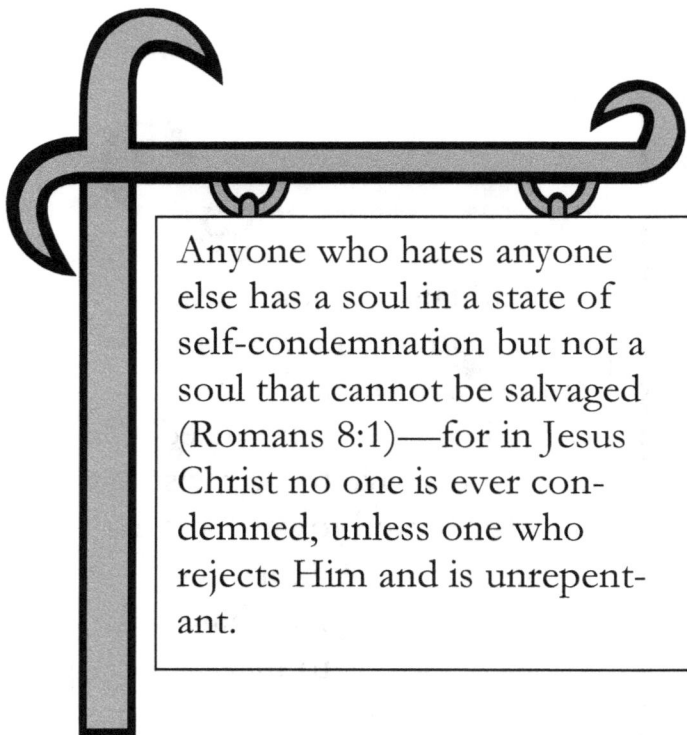

Anyone who hates anyone else has a soul in a state of self-condemnation but not a soul that cannot be salvaged (Romans 8:1)—for in Jesus Christ no one is ever condemned, unless one who rejects Him and is unrepentant.

64

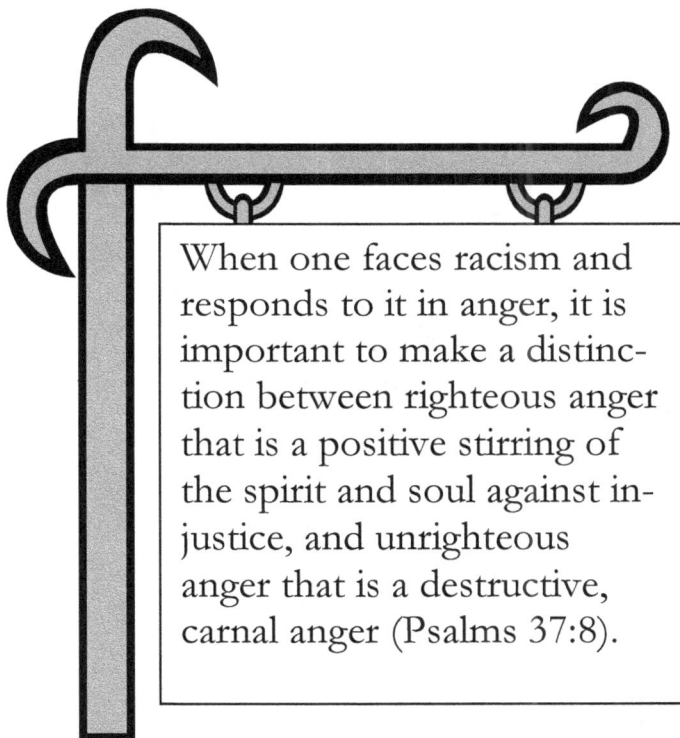

When one faces racism and responds to it in anger, it is important to make a distinction between righteous anger that is a positive stirring of the spirit and soul against injustice, and unrighteous anger that is a destructive, carnal anger (Psalms 37:8).

65

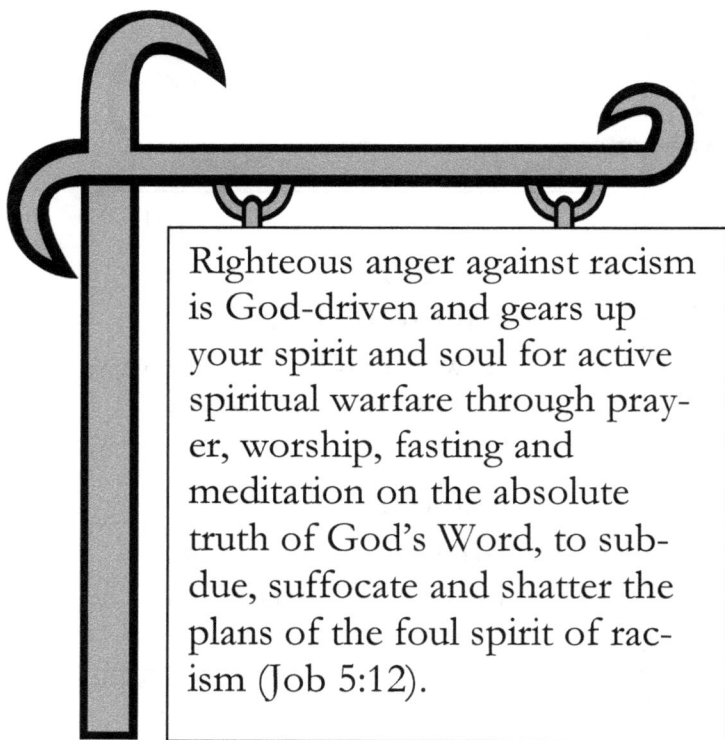

Righteous anger against racism is God-driven and gears up your spirit and soul for active spiritual warfare through prayer, worship, fasting and meditation on the absolute truth of God's Word, to subdue, suffocate and shatter the plans of the foul spirit of racism (Job 5:12).

66

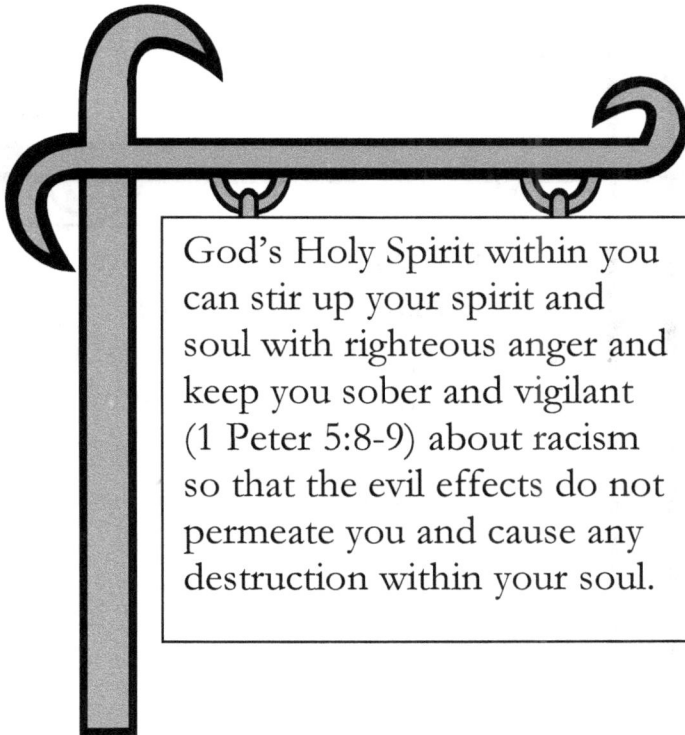

God's Holy Spirit within you can stir up your spirit and soul with righteous anger and keep you sober and vigilant (1 Peter 5:8-9) about racism so that the evil effects do not permeate you and cause any destruction within your soul.

67

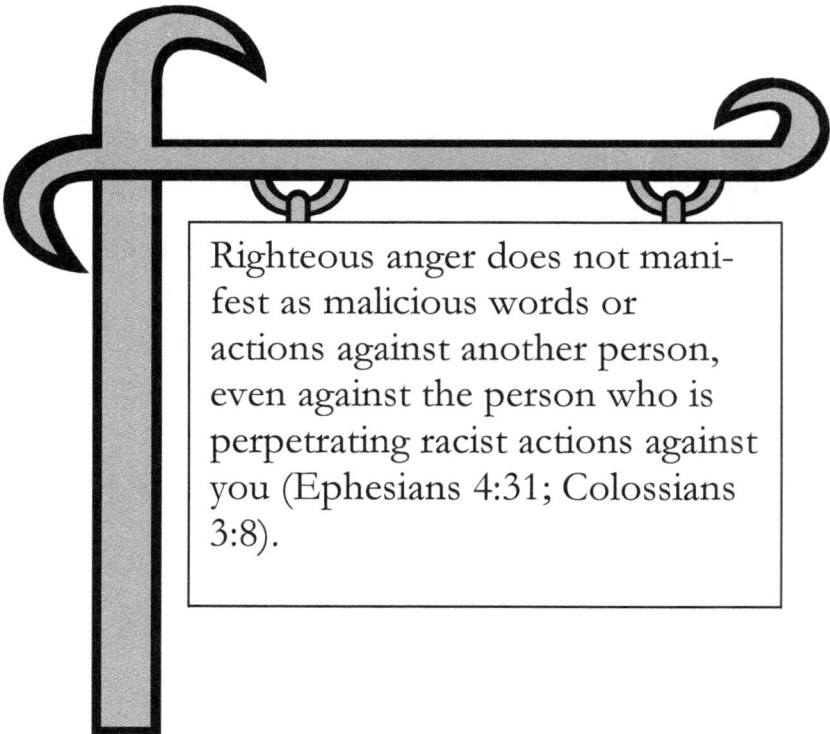

Righteous anger does not manifest as malicious words or actions against another person, even against the person who is perpetrating racist actions against you (Ephesians 4:31; Colossians 3:8).

68

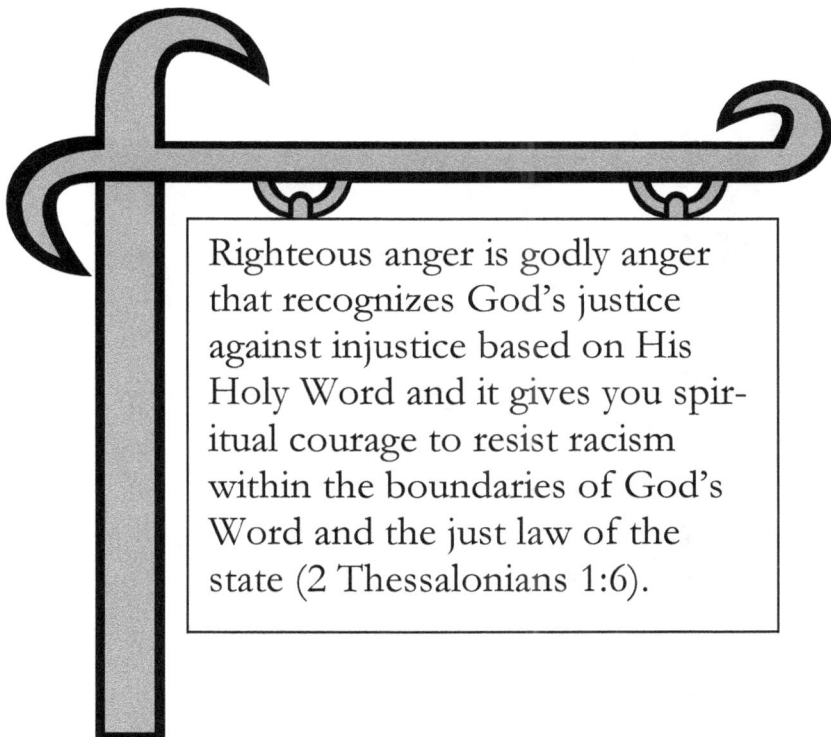

Righteous anger is godly anger that recognizes God's justice against injustice based on His Holy Word and it gives you spiritual courage to resist racism within the boundaries of God's Word and the just law of the state (2 Thessalonians 1:6).

69

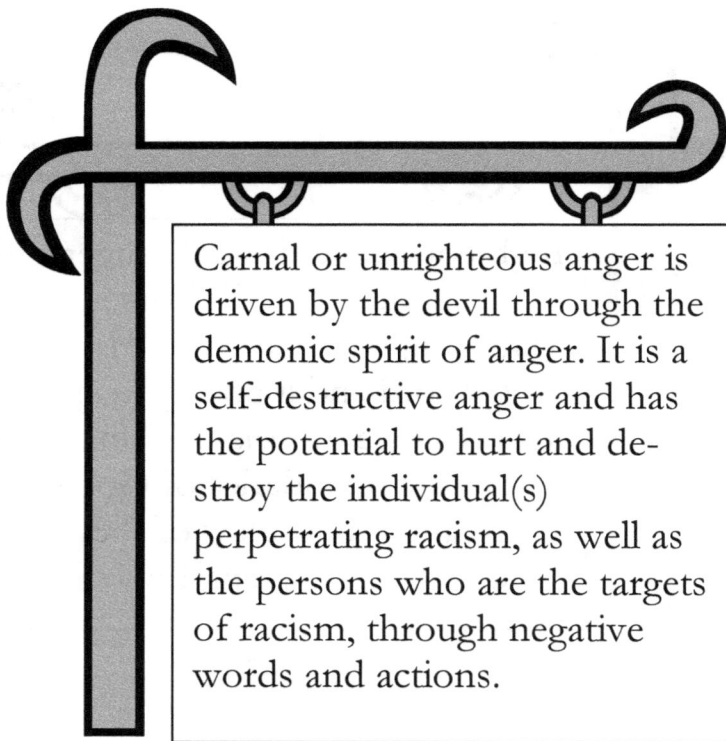

Carnal or unrighteous anger is driven by the devil through the demonic spirit of anger. It is a self-destructive anger and has the potential to hurt and destroy the individual(s) perpetrating racism, as well as the persons who are the targets of racism, through negative words and actions.

70

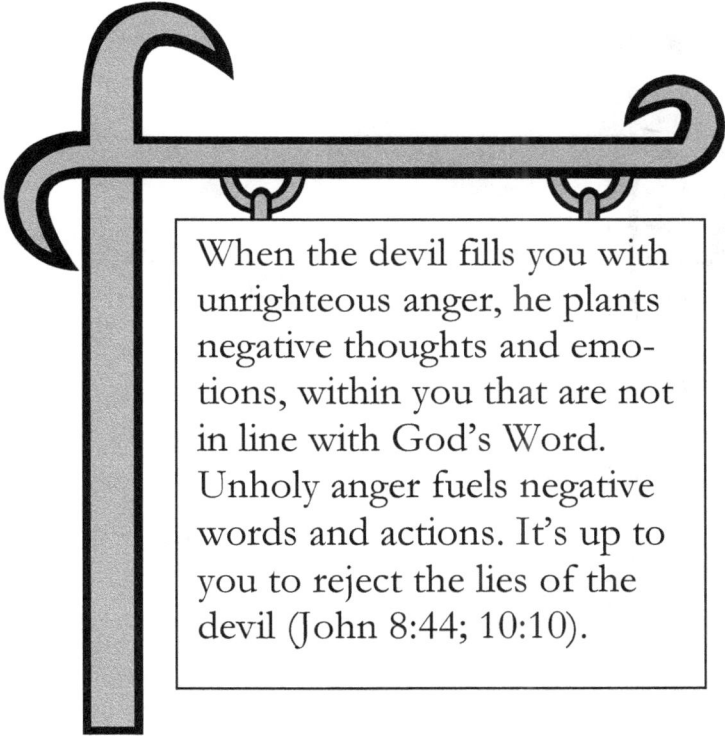

When the devil fills you with unrighteous anger, he plants negative thoughts and emotions, within you that are not in line with God's Word. Unholy anger fuels negative words and actions. It's up to you to reject the lies of the devil (John 8:44; 10:10).

71

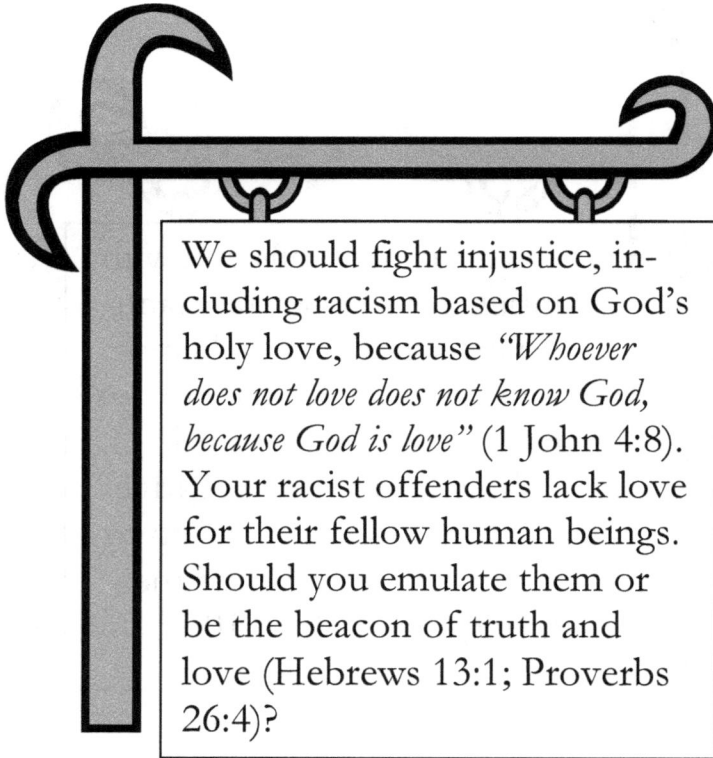

We should fight injustice, including racism based on God's holy love, because *"Whoever does not love does not know God, because God is love"* (1 John 4:8). Your racist offenders lack love for their fellow human beings. Should you emulate them or be the beacon of truth and love (Hebrews 13:1; Proverbs 26:4)?

72

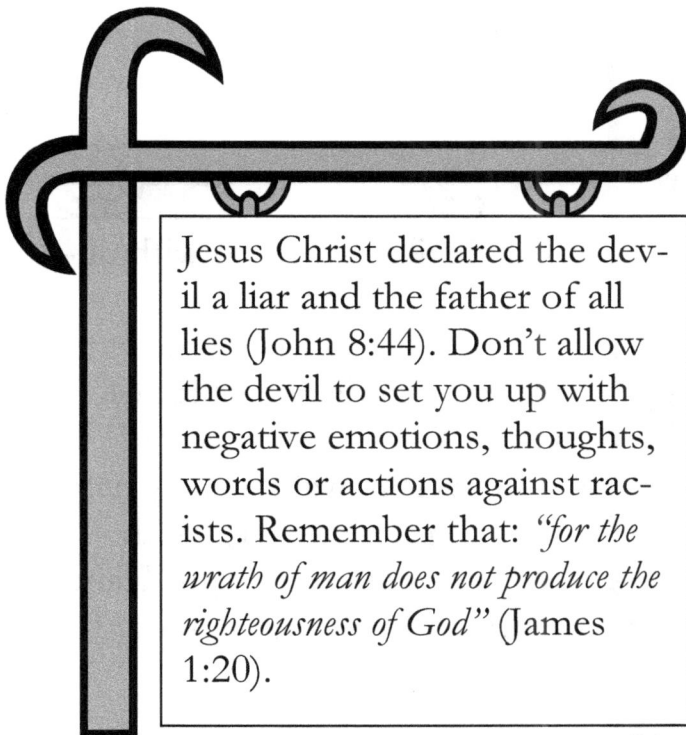

Jesus Christ declared the devil a liar and the father of all lies (John 8:44). Don't allow the devil to set you up with negative emotions, thoughts, words or actions against racists. Remember that: *"for the wrath of man does not produce the righteousness of God"* (James 1:20).

73

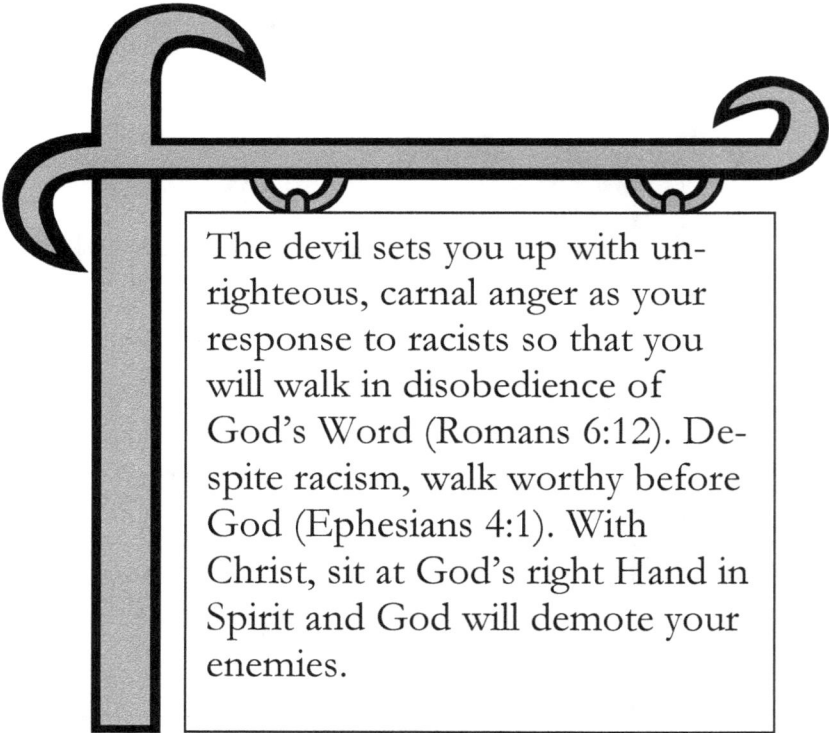

The devil sets you up with unrighteous, carnal anger as your response to racists so that you will walk in disobedience of God's Word (Romans 6:12). Despite racism, walk worthy before God (Ephesians 4:1). With Christ, sit at God's right Hand in Spirit and God will demote your enemies.

74

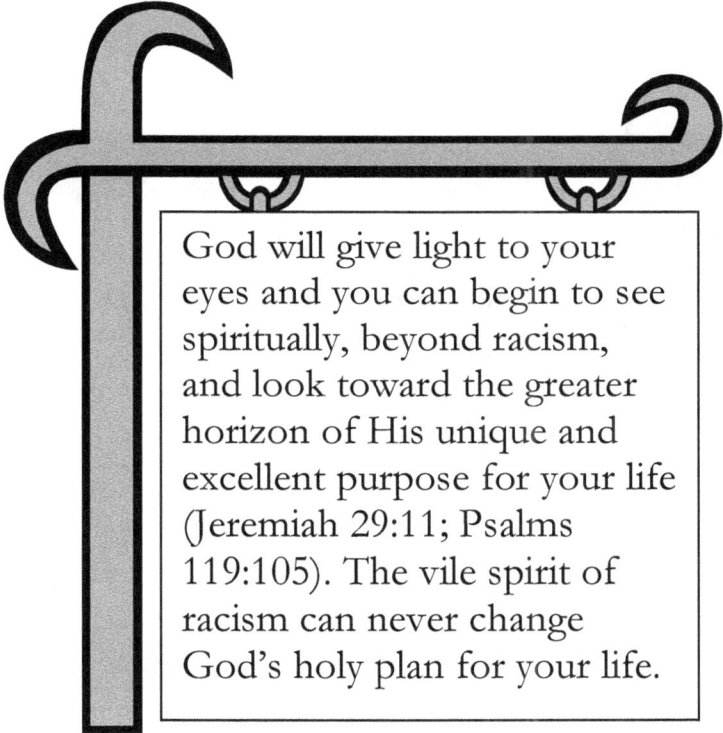

God will give light to your eyes and you can begin to see spiritually, beyond racism, and look toward the greater horizon of His unique and excellent purpose for your life (Jeremiah 29:11; Psalms 119:105). The vile spirit of racism can never change God's holy plan for your life.

75

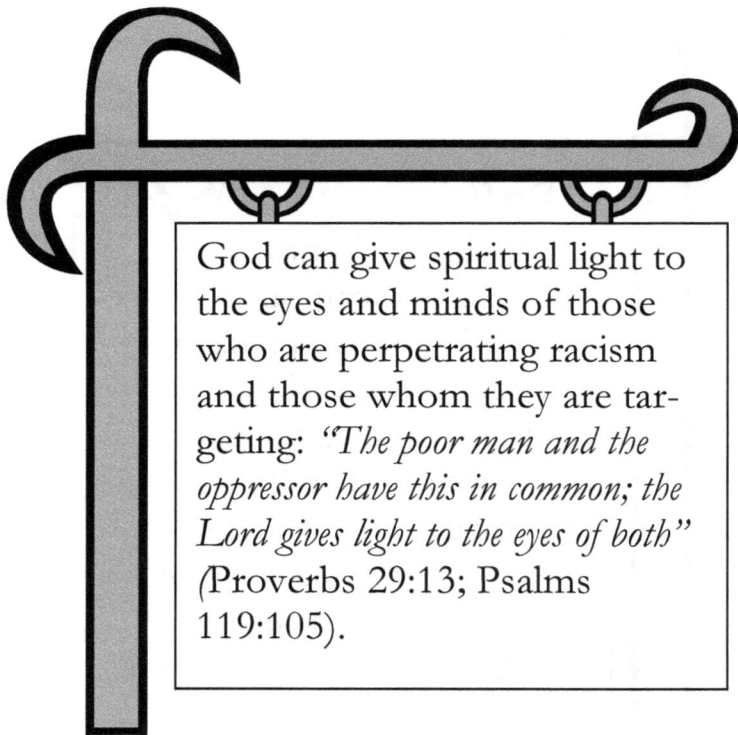

God can give spiritual light to the eyes and minds of those who are perpetrating racism and those whom they are targeting: *"The poor man and the oppressor have this in common; the Lord gives light to the eyes of both"* (Proverbs 29:13; Psalms 119:105).

76

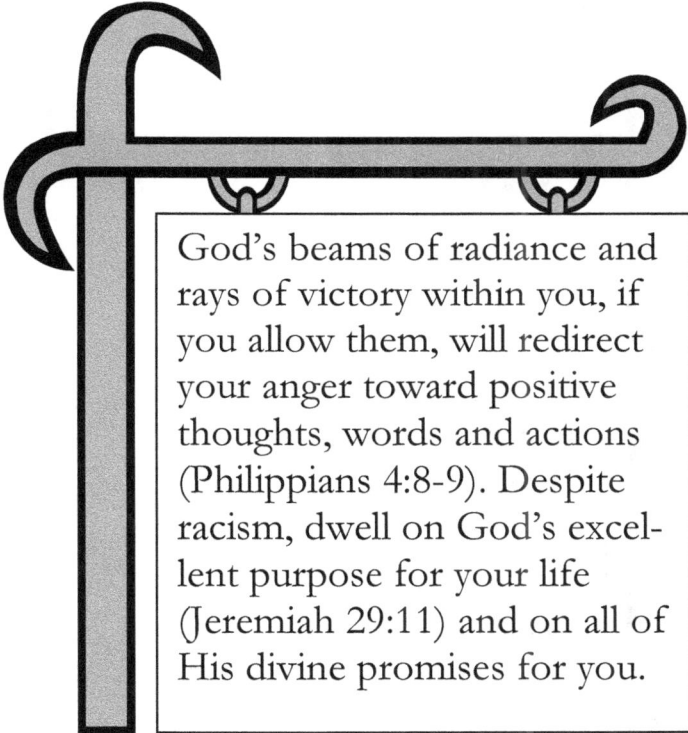

God's beams of radiance and rays of victory within you, if you allow them, will redirect your anger toward positive thoughts, words and actions (Philippians 4:8-9). Despite racism, dwell on God's excellent purpose for your life (Jeremiah 29:11) and on all of His divine promises for you.

77

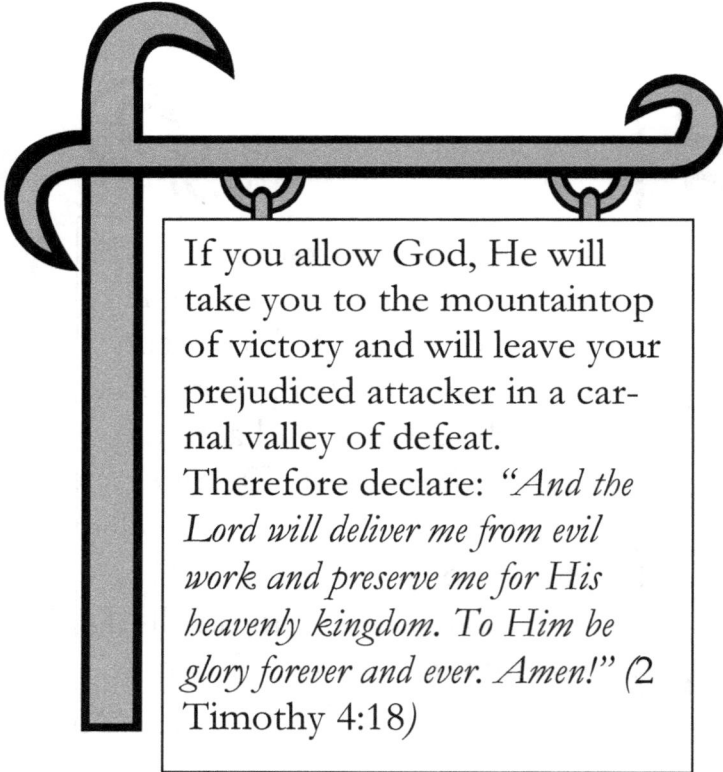

If you allow God, He will take you to the mountaintop of victory and will leave your prejudiced attacker in a carnal valley of defeat.
Therefore declare: *"And the Lord will deliver me from evil work and preserve me for His heavenly kingdom. To Him be glory forever and ever. Amen!"* (2 Timothy 4:18)

78

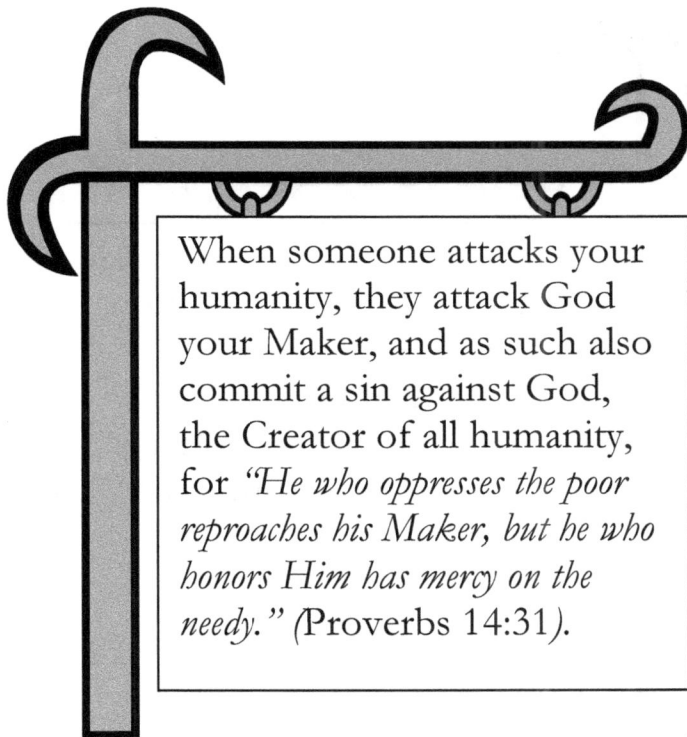

When someone attacks your humanity, they attack God your Maker, and as such also commit a sin against God, the Creator of all humanity, for *"He who oppresses the poor reproaches his Maker, but he who honors Him has mercy on the needy."* (Proverbs 14:31).

79

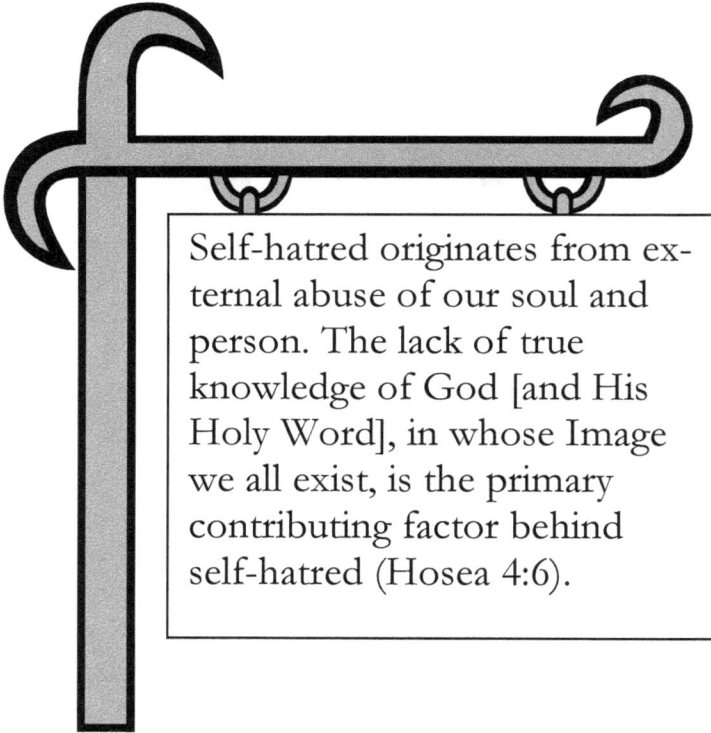

Self-hatred originates from ex-ternal abuse of our soul and person. The lack of true knowledge of God [and His Holy Word], in whose Image we all exist, is the primary contributing factor behind self-hatred (Hosea 4:6).

80

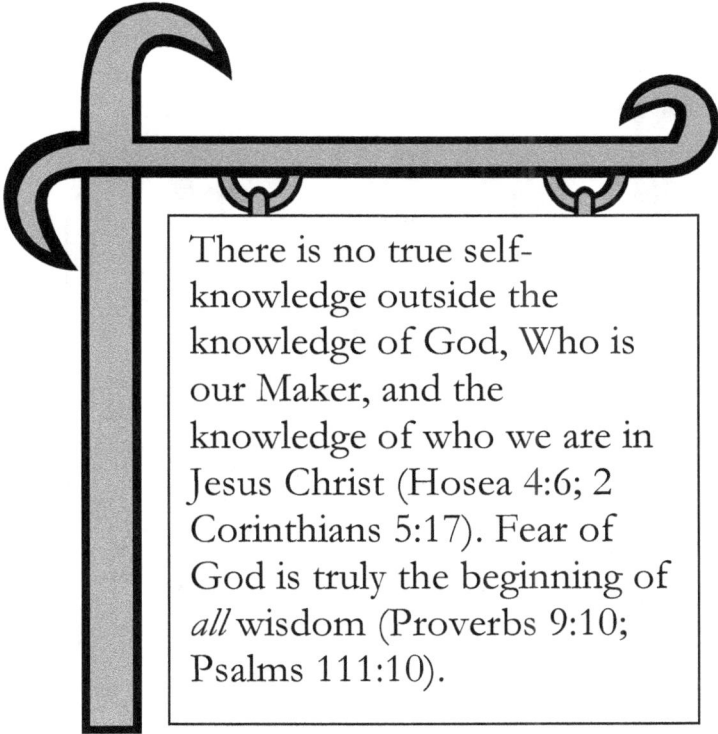

There is no true self-knowledge outside the knowledge of God, Who is our Maker, and the knowledge of who we are in Jesus Christ (Hosea 4:6; 2 Corinthians 5:17). Fear of God is truly the beginning of *all* wisdom (Proverbs 9:10; Psalms 111:10).

81

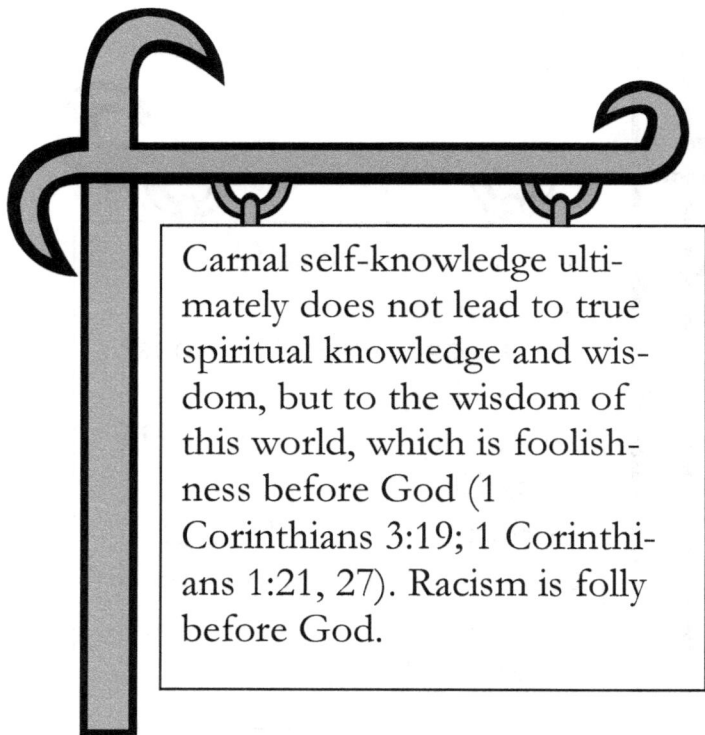

Carnal self-knowledge ultimately does not lead to true spiritual knowledge and wisdom, but to the wisdom of this world, which is foolishness before God (1 Corinthians 3:19; 1 Corinthians 1:21, 27). Racism is folly before God.

82

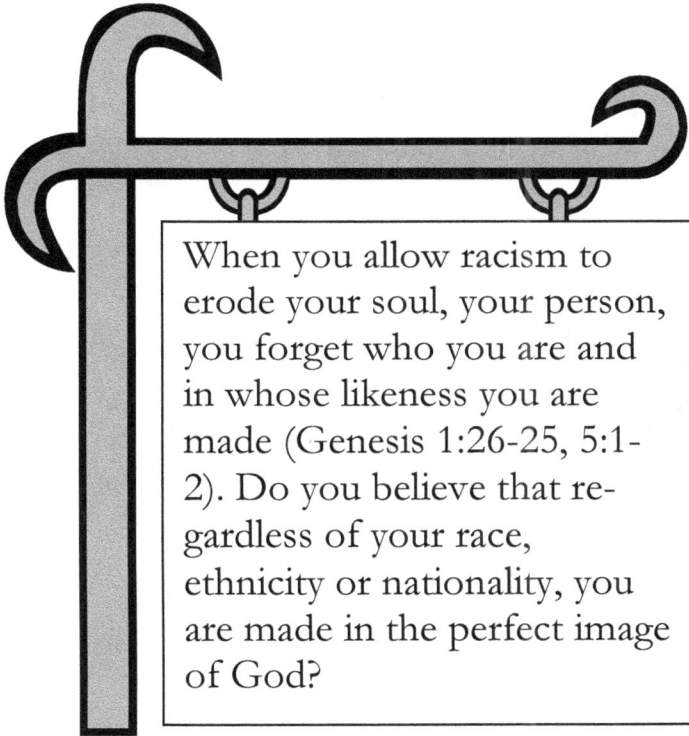

When you allow racism to erode your soul, your person, you forget who you are and in whose likeness you are made (Genesis 1:26-25, 5:1-2). Do you believe that regardless of your race, ethnicity or nationality, you are made in the perfect image of God?

83

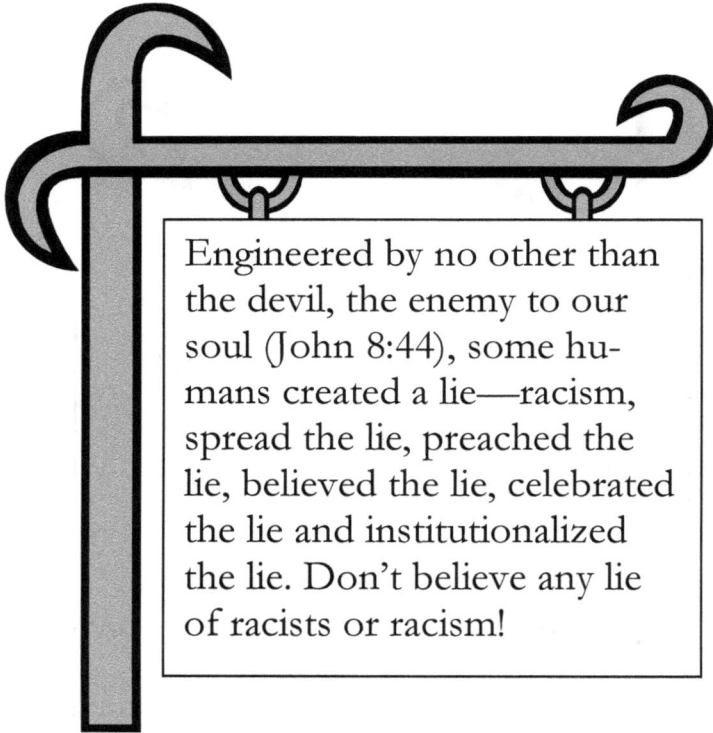

Engineered by no other than the devil, the enemy to our soul (John 8:44), some humans created a lie—racism, spread the lie, preached the lie, believed the lie, celebrated the lie and institutionalized the lie. Don't believe any lie of racists or racism!

84

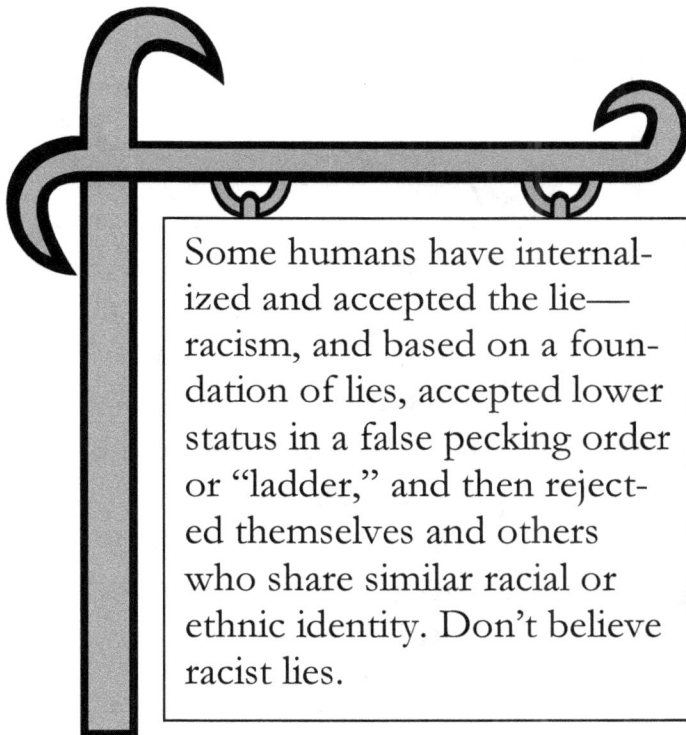

Some humans have internalized and accepted the lie—racism, and based on a foundation of lies, accepted lower status in a false pecking order or "ladder," and then rejected themselves and others who share similar racial or ethnic identity. Don't believe racist lies.

85

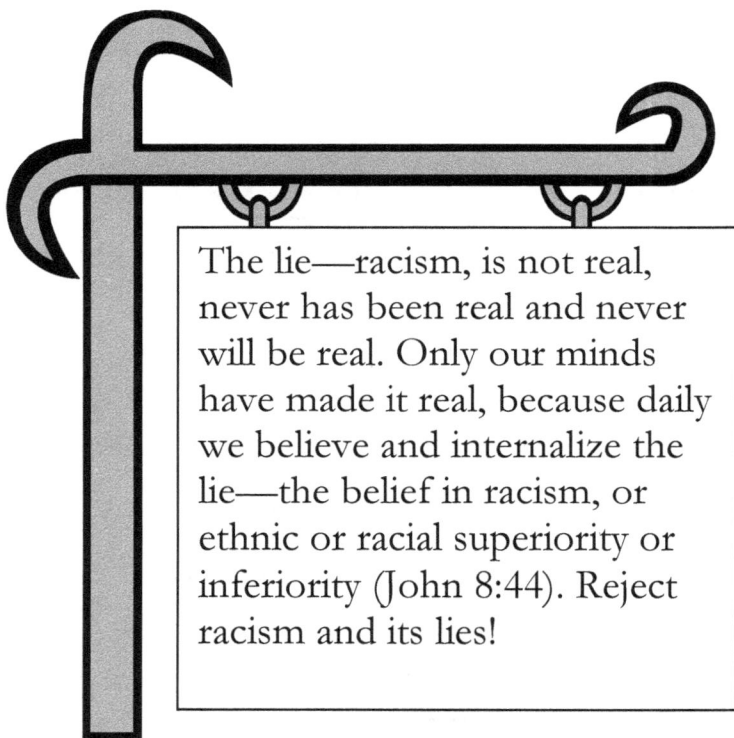

The lie—racism, is not real, never has been real and never will be real. Only our minds have made it real, because daily we believe and internalize the lie—the belief in racism, or ethnic or racial superiority or inferiority (John 8:44). Reject racism and its lies!

86

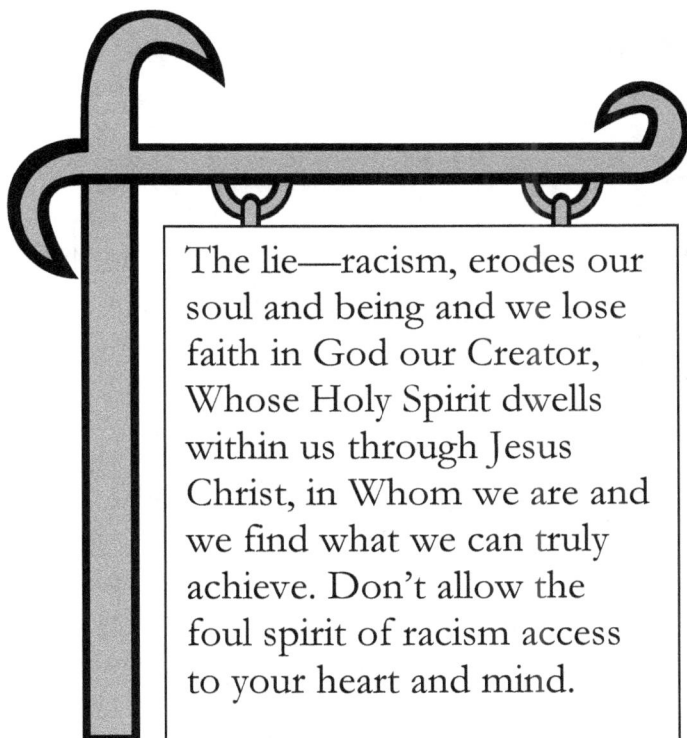

The lie—racism, erodes our soul and being and we lose faith in God our Creator, Whose Holy Spirit dwells within us through Jesus Christ, in Whom we are and we find what we can truly achieve. Don't allow the foul spirit of racism access to your heart and mind.

87

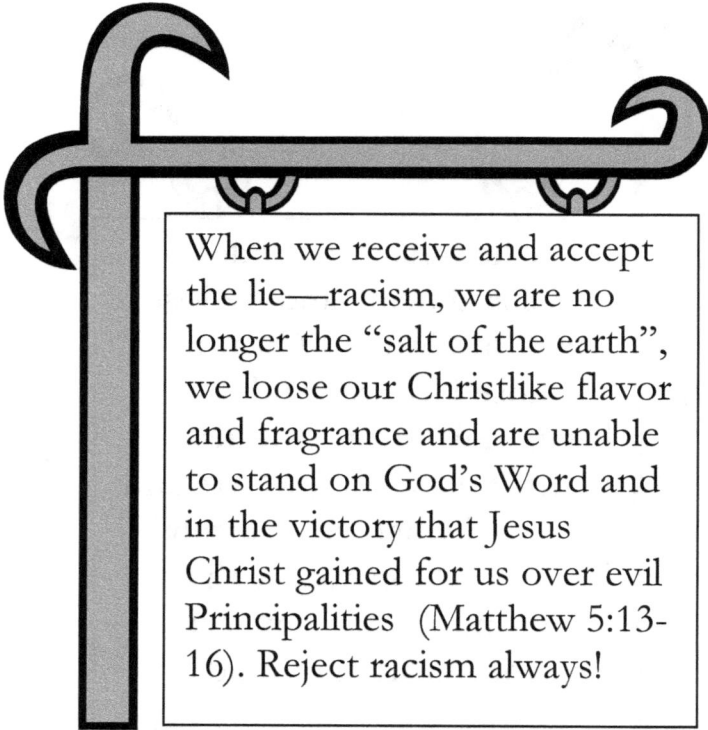

When we receive and accept the lie—racism, we are no longer the "salt of the earth", we loose our Christlike flavor and fragrance and are unable to stand on God's Word and in the victory that Jesus Christ gained for us over evil Principalities (Matthew 5:13-16). Reject racism always!

88

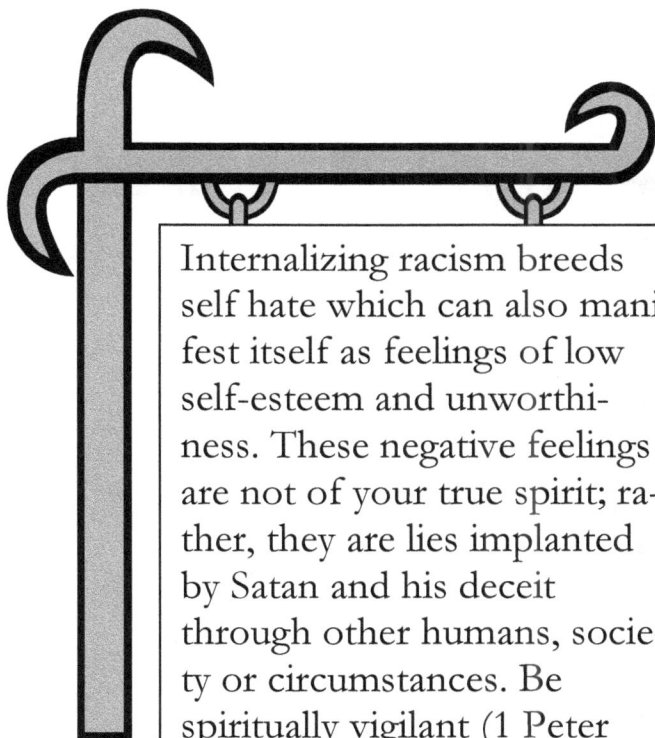

Internalizing racism breeds self hate which can also manifest itself as feelings of low self-esteem and unworthiness. These negative feelings are not of your true spirit; rather, they are lies implanted by Satan and his deceit through other humans, society or circumstances. Be spiritually vigilant (1 Peter 5:8).

89

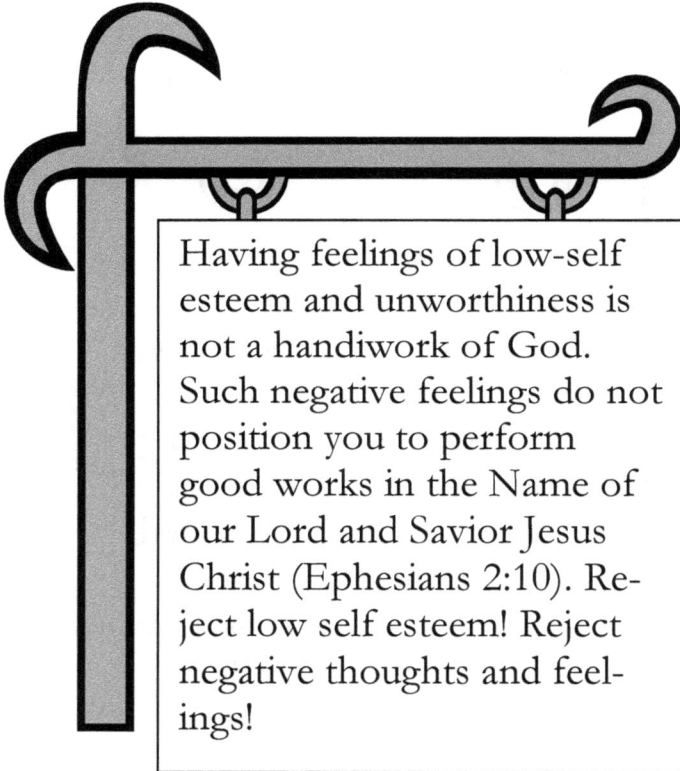

Having feelings of low-self esteem and unworthiness is not a handiwork of God. Such negative feelings do not position you to perform good works in the Name of our Lord and Savior Jesus Christ (Ephesians 2:10). Reject low self esteem! Reject negative thoughts and feelings!

90

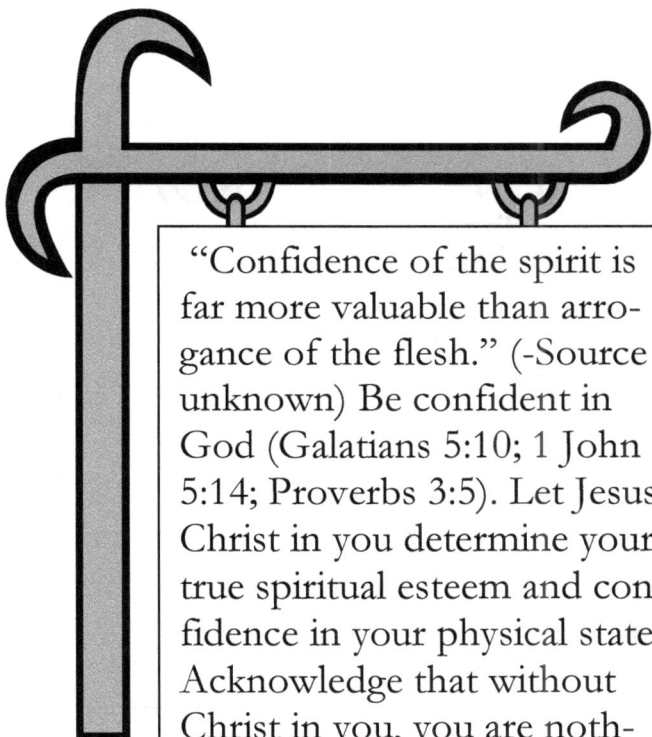

"Confidence of the spirit is far more valuable than arrogance of the flesh." (-Source unknown) Be confident in God (Galatians 5:10; 1 John 5:14; Proverbs 3:5). Let Jesus Christ in you determine your true spiritual esteem and confidence in your physical state. Acknowledge that without Christ in you, you are nothing!

91

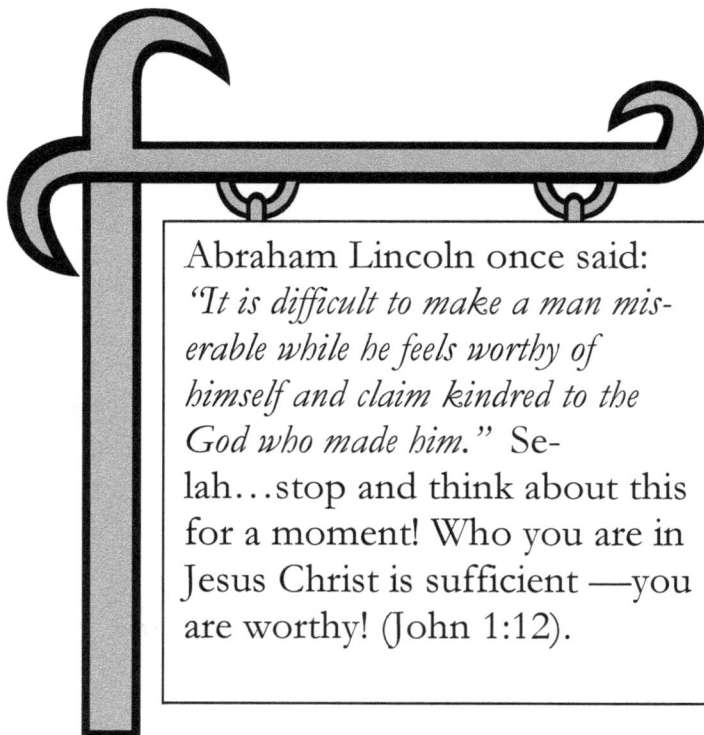

Abraham Lincoln once said: *"It is difficult to make a man miserable while he feels worthy of himself and claim kindred to the God who made him."* Selah…stop and think about this for a moment! Who you are in Jesus Christ is sufficient —you are worthy! (John 1:12).

92

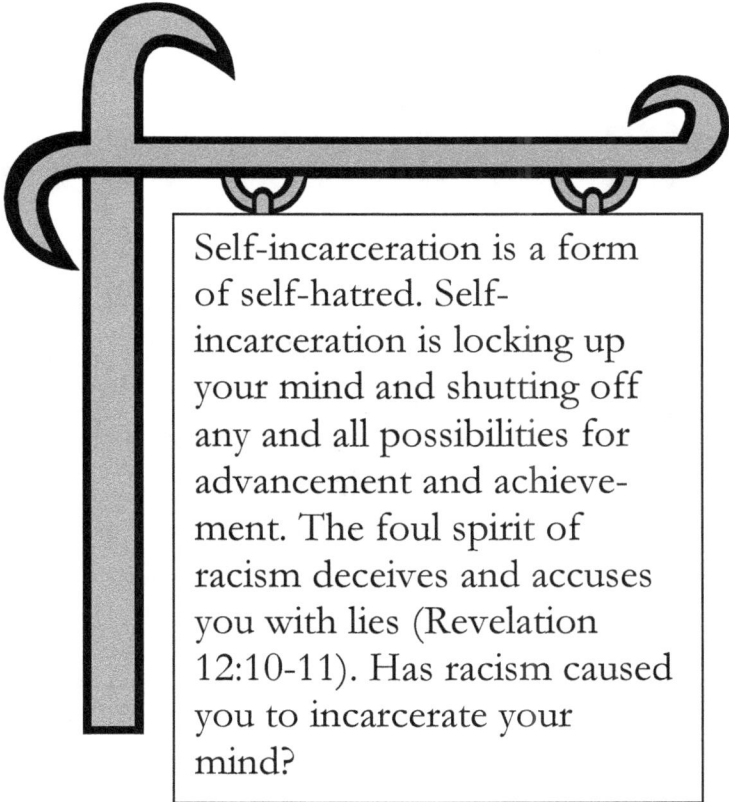

Self-incarceration is a form of self-hatred. Self-incarceration is locking up your mind and shutting off any and all possibilities for advancement and achievement. The foul spirit of racism deceives and accuses you with lies (Revelation 12:10-11). Has racism caused you to incarcerate your mind?

93

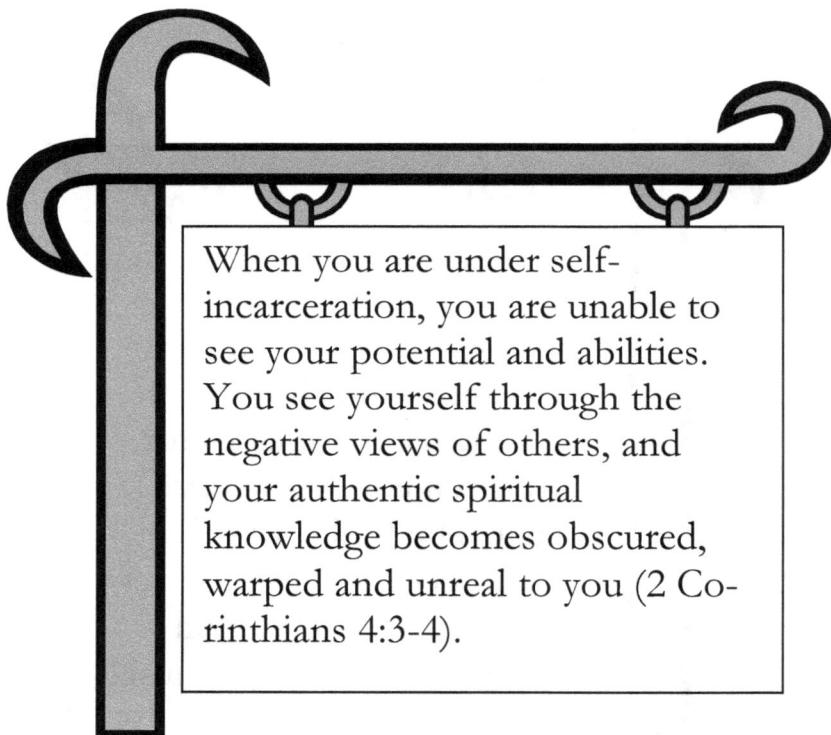

When you are under self-incarceration, you are unable to see your potential and abilities. You see yourself through the negative views of others, and your authentic spiritual knowledge becomes obscured, warped and unreal to you (2 Corinthians 4:3-4).

94

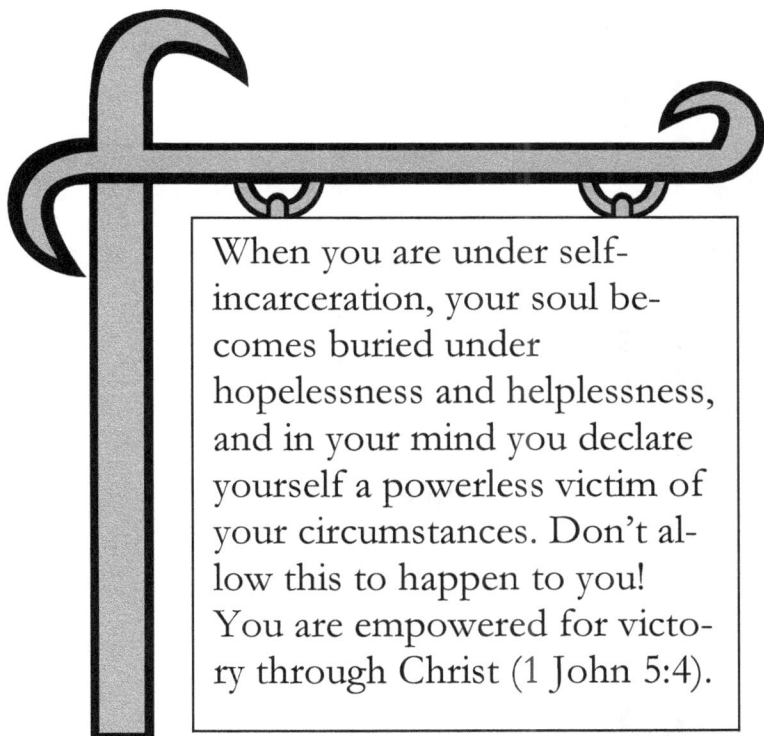

When you are under self-incarceration, your soul becomes buried under hopelessness and helplessness, and in your mind you declare yourself a powerless victim of your circumstances. Don't allow this to happen to you! You are empowered for victory through Christ (1 John 5:4).

95

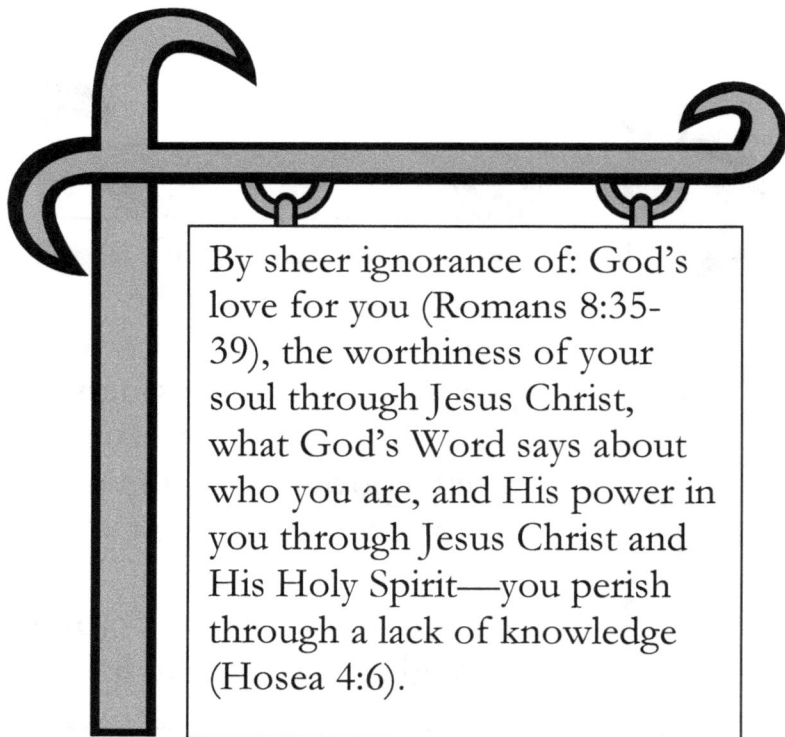

By sheer ignorance of: God's love for you (Romans 8:35-39), the worthiness of your soul through Jesus Christ, what God's Word says about who you are, and His power in you through Jesus Christ and His Holy Spirit—you perish through a lack of knowledge (Hosea 4:6).

96

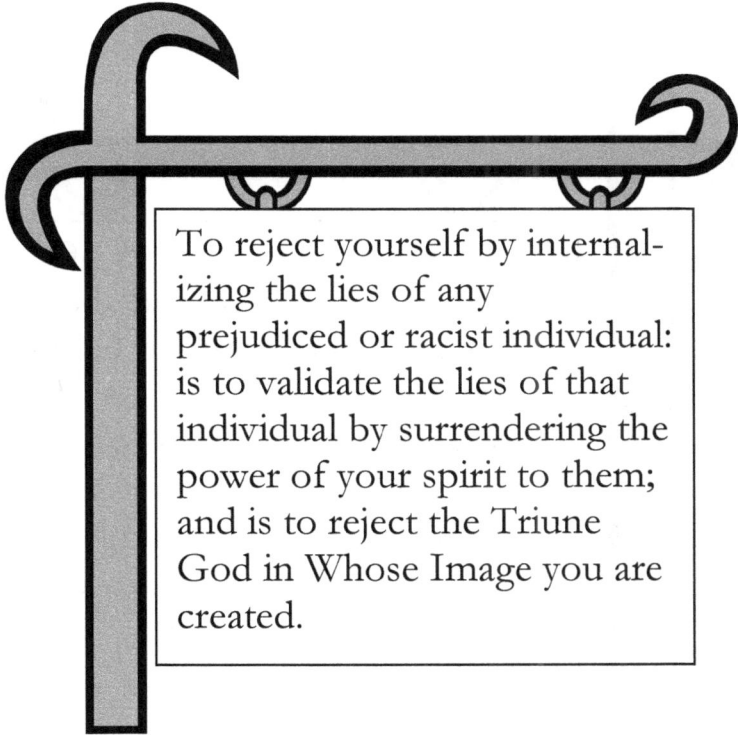

To reject yourself by internalizing the lies of any prejudiced or racist individual: is to validate the lies of that individual by surrendering the power of your spirit to them; and is to reject the Triune God in Whose Image you are created.

97

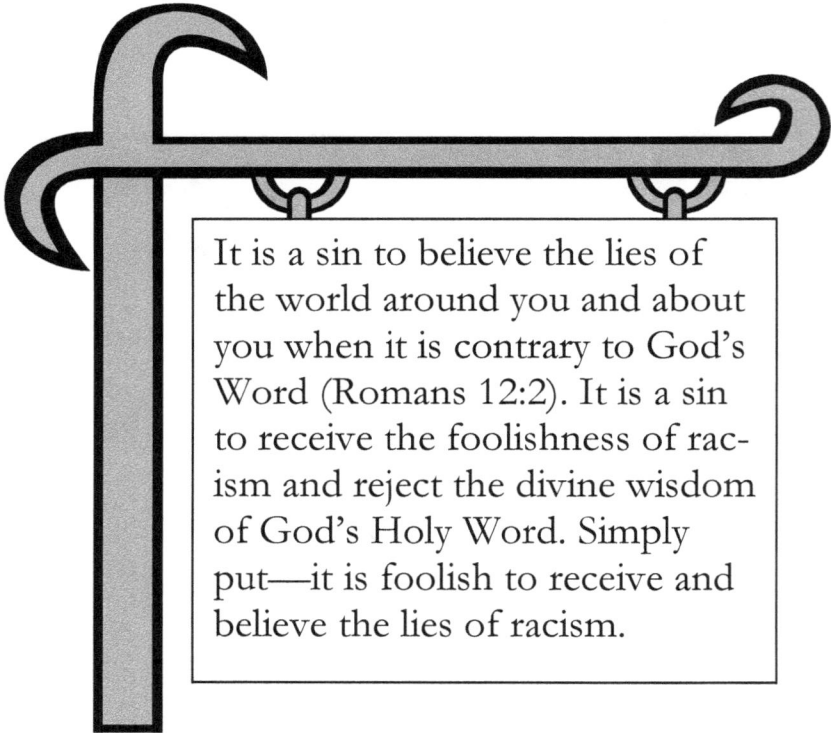

It is a sin to believe the lies of the world around you and about you when it is contrary to God's Word (Romans 12:2). It is a sin to receive the foolishness of racism and reject the divine wisdom of God's Holy Word. Simply put—it is foolish to receive and believe the lies of racism.

98

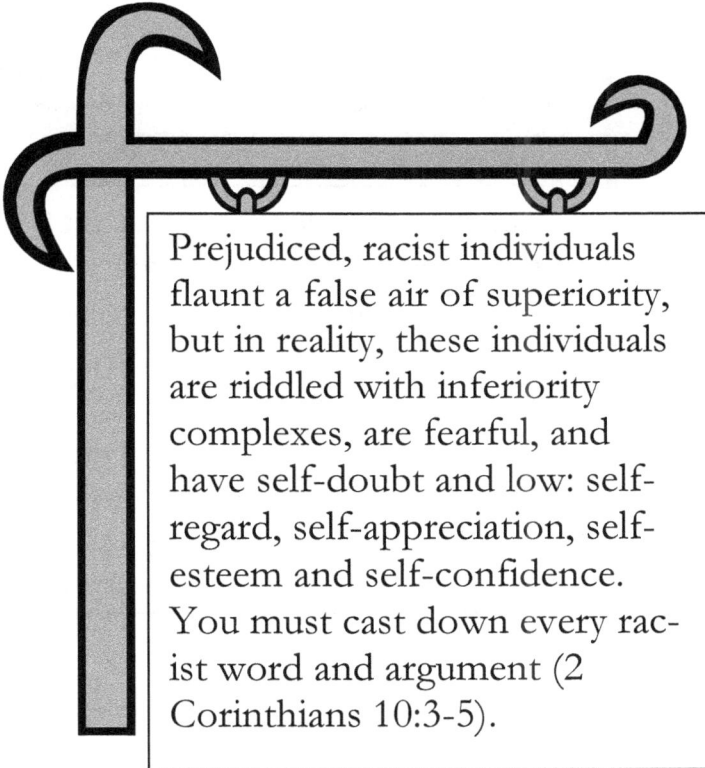

Prejudiced, racist individuals flaunt a false air of superiority, but in reality, these individuals are riddled with inferiority complexes, are fearful, and have self-doubt and low: self-regard, self-appreciation, self-esteem and self-confidence. You must cast down every racist word and argument (2 Corinthians 10:3-5).

99

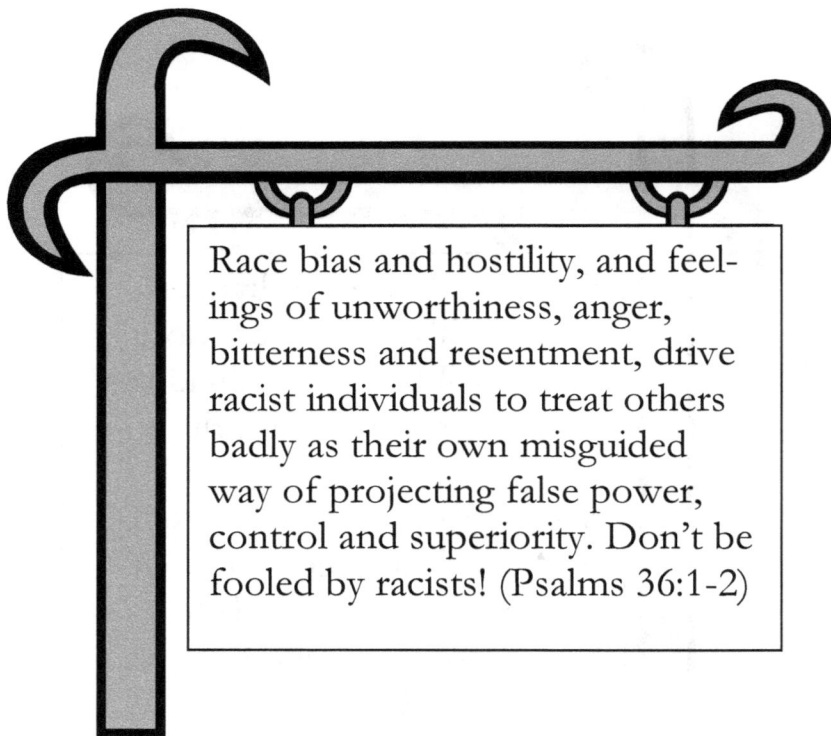

Race bias and hostility, and feelings of unworthiness, anger, bitterness and resentment, drive racist individuals to treat others badly as their own misguided way of projecting false power, control and superiority. Don't be fooled by racists! (Psalms 36:1-2)

100

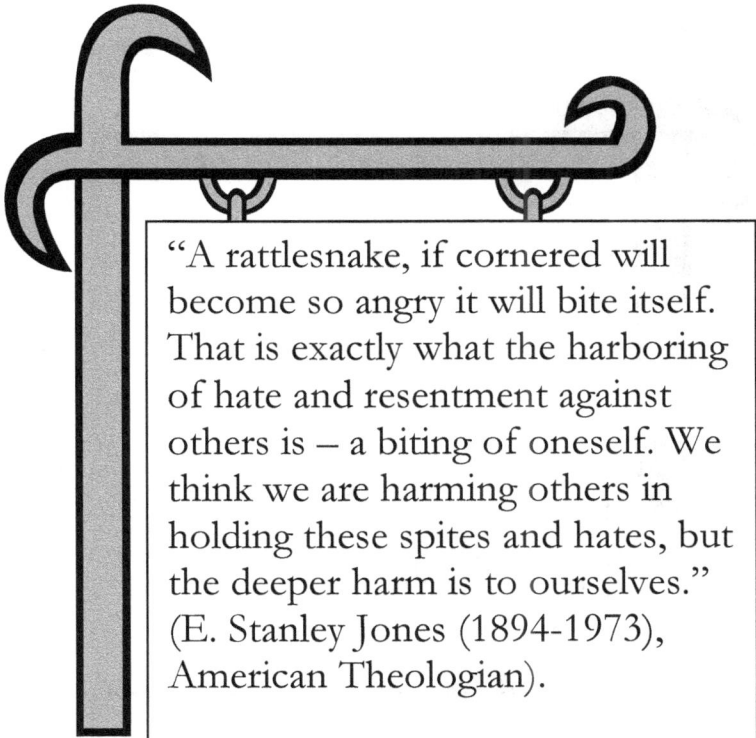

"A rattlesnake, if cornered will become so angry it will bite itself. That is exactly what the harboring of hate and resentment against others is – a biting of oneself. We think we are harming others in holding these spites and hates, but the deeper harm is to ourselves." (E. Stanley Jones (1894-1973), American Theologian).

101

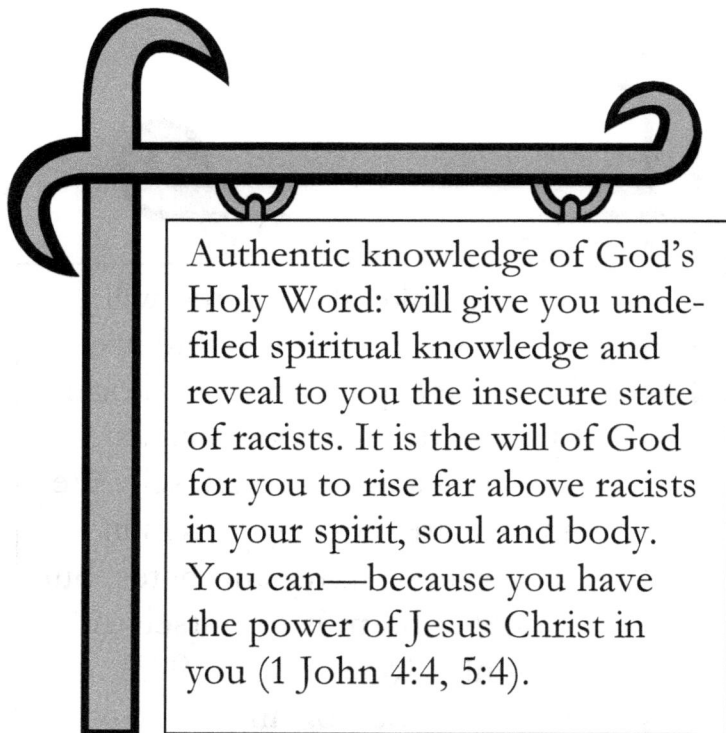

Authentic knowledge of God's Holy Word: will give you unde-filed spiritual knowledge and reveal to you the insecure state of racists. It is the will of God for you to rise far above racists in your spirit, soul and body. You can—because you have the power of Jesus Christ in you (1 John 4:4, 5:4).

102

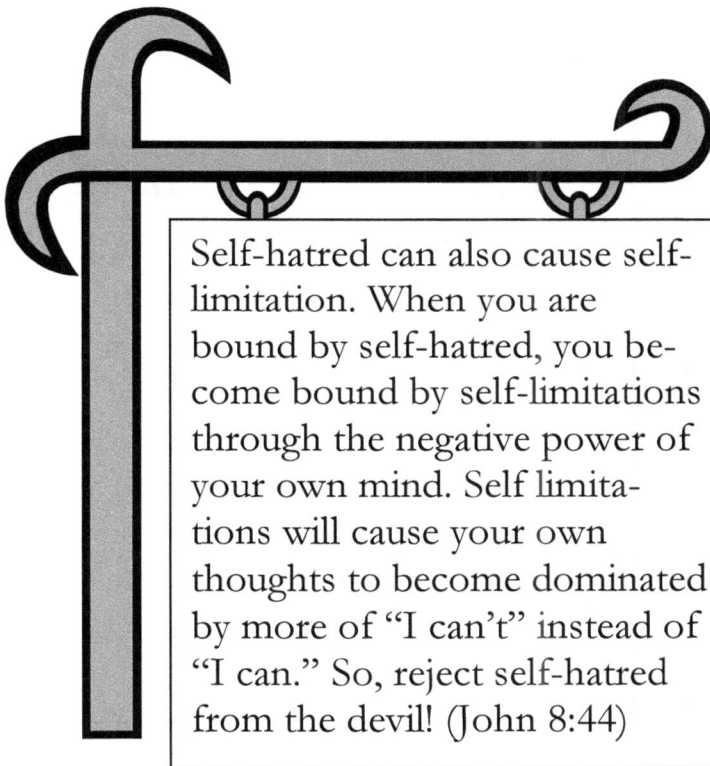

Self-hatred can also cause self-limitation. When you are bound by self-hatred, you become bound by self-limitations through the negative power of your own mind. Self limitations will cause your own thoughts to become dominated by more of "I can't" instead of "I can." So, reject self-hatred from the devil! (John 8:44)

103

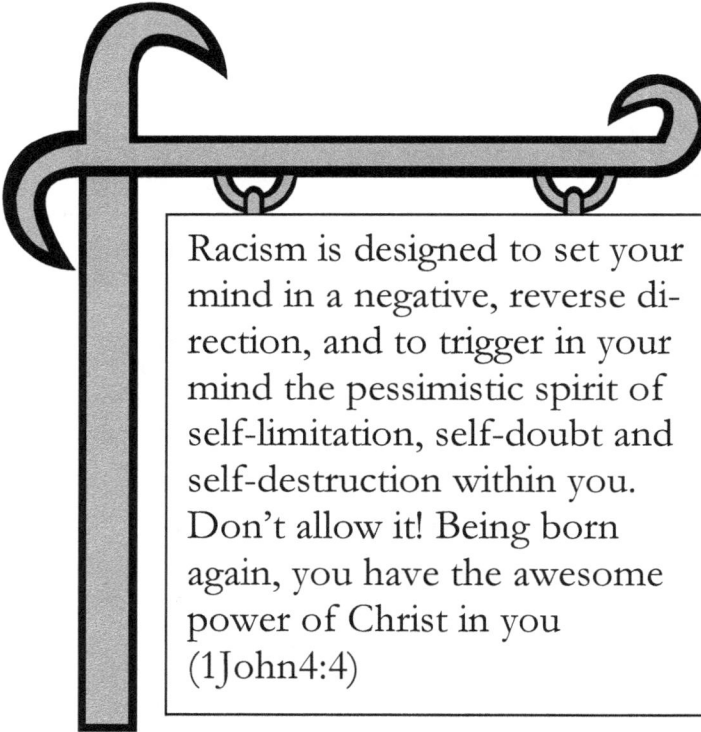

Racism is designed to set your mind in a negative, reverse direction, and to trigger in your mind the pessimistic spirit of self-limitation, self-doubt and self-destruction within you. Don't allow it! Being born again, you have the awesome power of Christ in you (1John4:4)

104

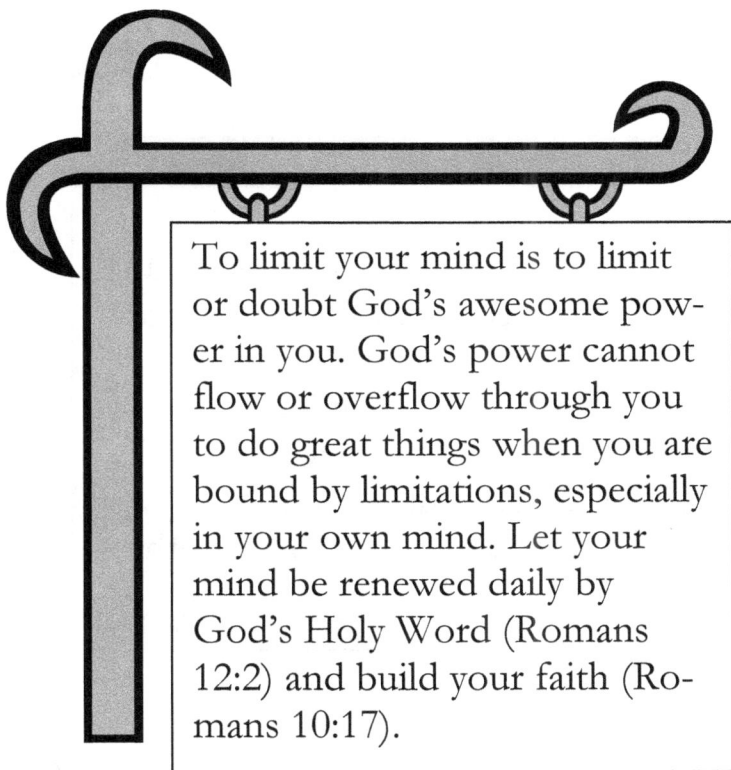

To limit your mind is to limit or doubt God's awesome power in you. God's power cannot flow or overflow through you to do great things when you are bound by limitations, especially in your own mind. Let your mind be renewed daily by God's Holy Word (Romans 12:2) and build your faith (Romans 10:17).

105

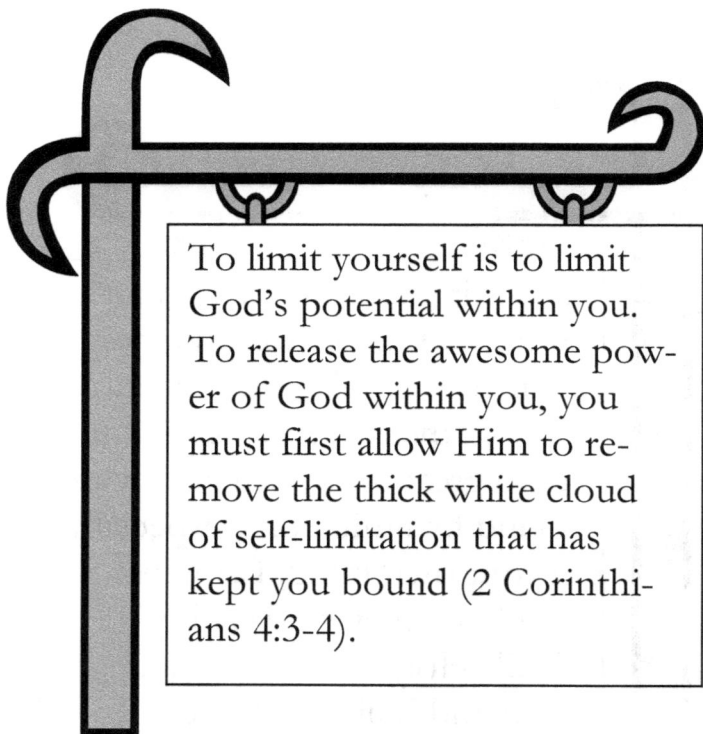

To limit yourself is to limit God's potential within you. To release the awesome power of God within you, you must first allow Him to remove the thick white cloud of self-limitation that has kept you bound (2 Corinthians 4:3-4).

106

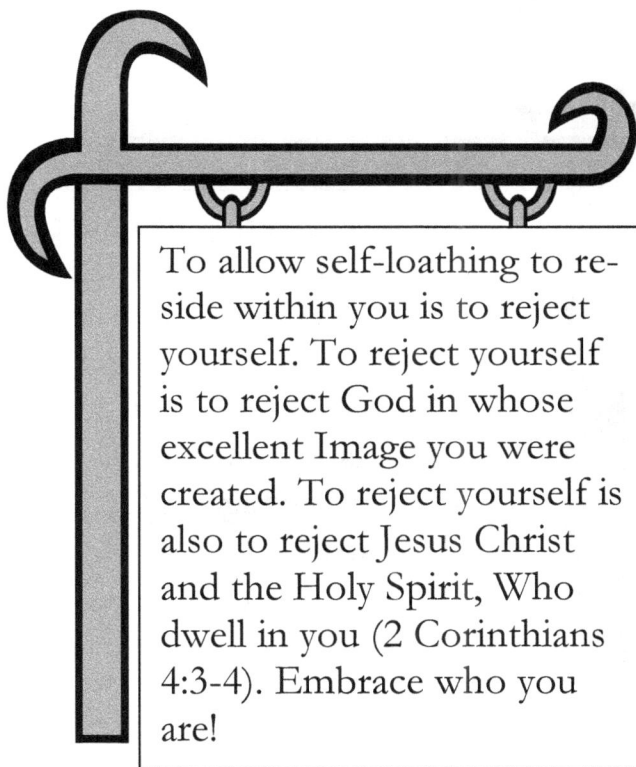

To allow self-loathing to reside within you is to reject yourself. To reject yourself is to reject God in whose excellent Image you were created. To reject yourself is also to reject Jesus Christ and the Holy Spirit, Who dwell in you (2 Corinthians 4:3-4). Embrace who you are!

107

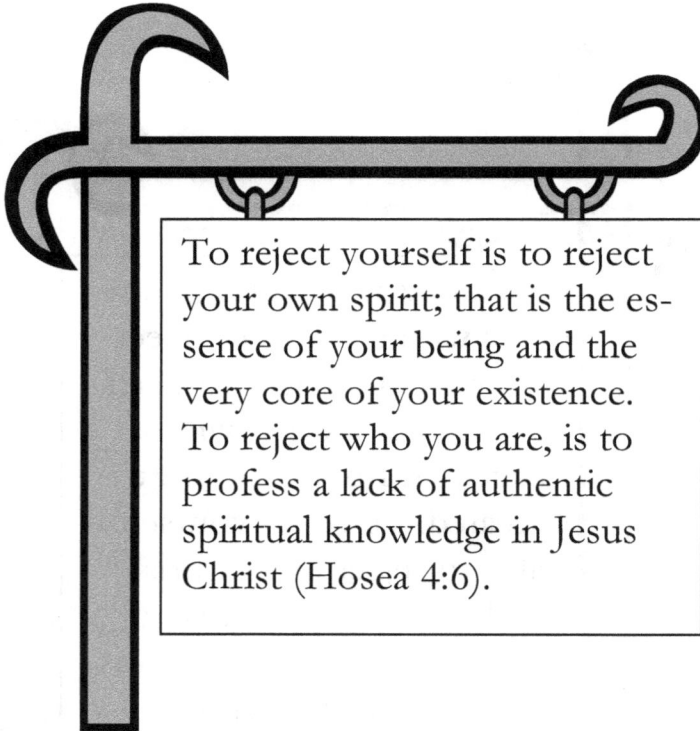

To reject yourself is to reject your own spirit; that is the essence of your being and the very core of your existence. To reject who you are, is to profess a lack of authentic spiritual knowledge in Jesus Christ (Hosea 4:6).

108

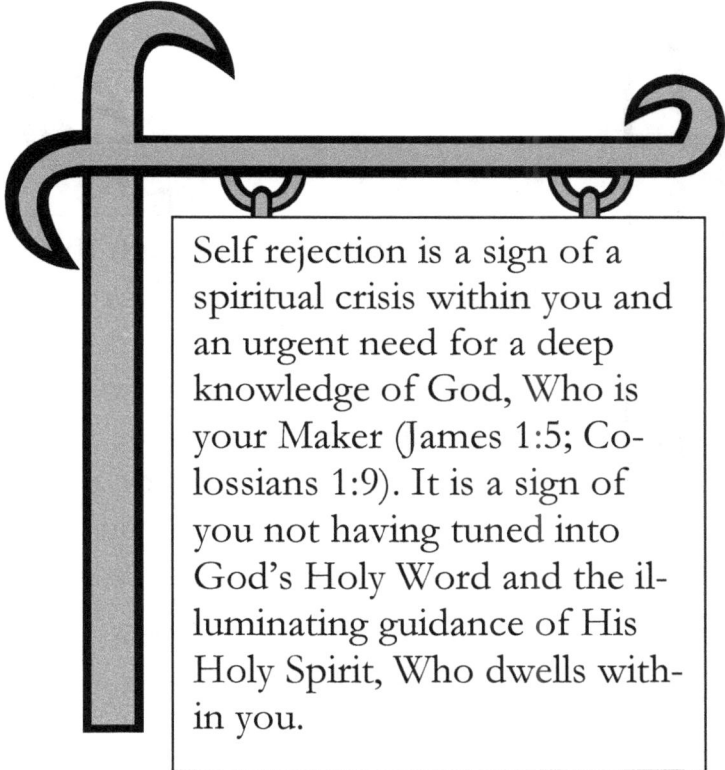

Self rejection is a sign of a spiritual crisis within you and an urgent need for a deep knowledge of God, Who is your Maker (James 1:5; Colossians 1:9). It is a sign of you not having tuned into God's Holy Word and the illuminating guidance of His Holy Spirit, Who dwells within you.

109

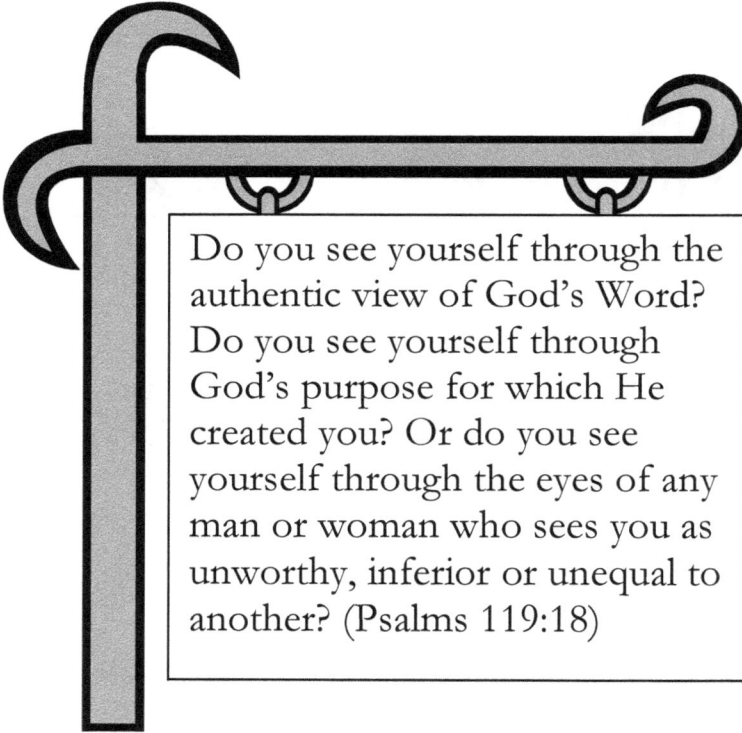

Do you see yourself through the authentic view of God's Word? Do you see yourself through God's purpose for which He created you? Or do you see yourself through the eyes of any man or woman who sees you as unworthy, inferior or unequal to another? (Psalms 119:18)

110

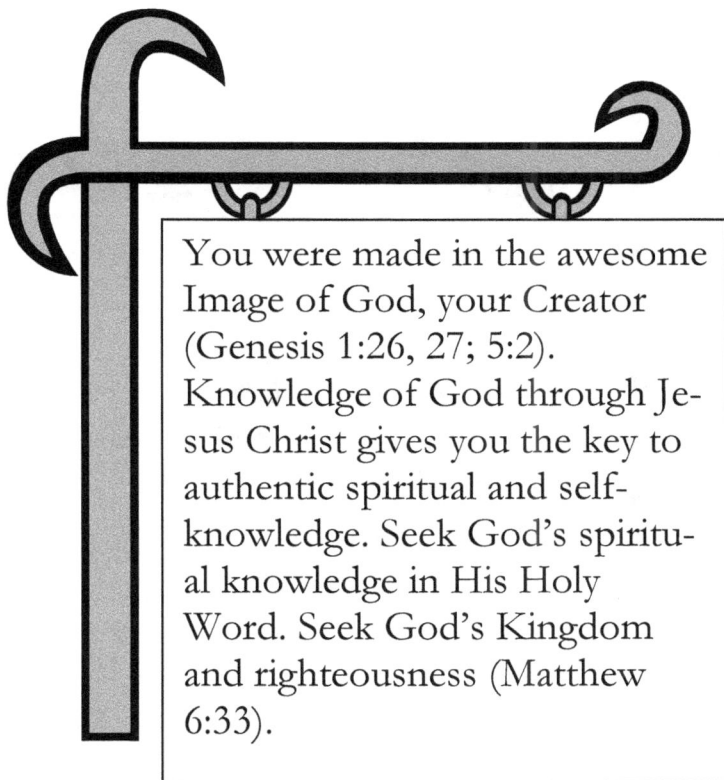

You were made in the awesome Image of God, your Creator (Genesis 1:26, 27; 5:2). Knowledge of God through Jesus Christ gives you the key to authentic spiritual and self-knowledge. Seek God's spiritual knowledge in His Holy Word. Seek God's Kingdom and righteousness (Matthew 6:33).

111

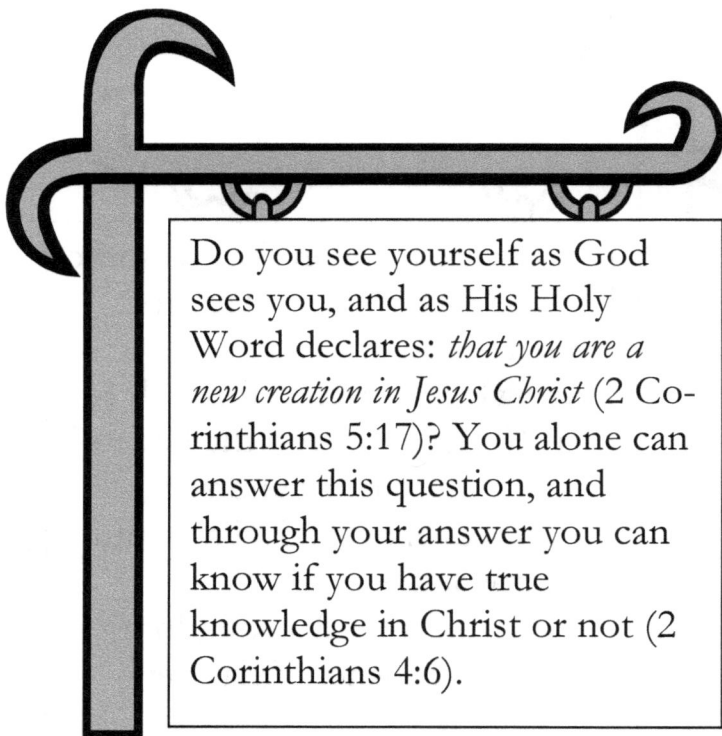

Do you see yourself as God sees you, and as His Holy Word declares: *that you are a new creation in Jesus Christ* (2 Corinthians 5:17)? You alone can answer this question, and through your answer you can know if you have true knowledge in Christ or not (2 Corinthians 4:6).

112

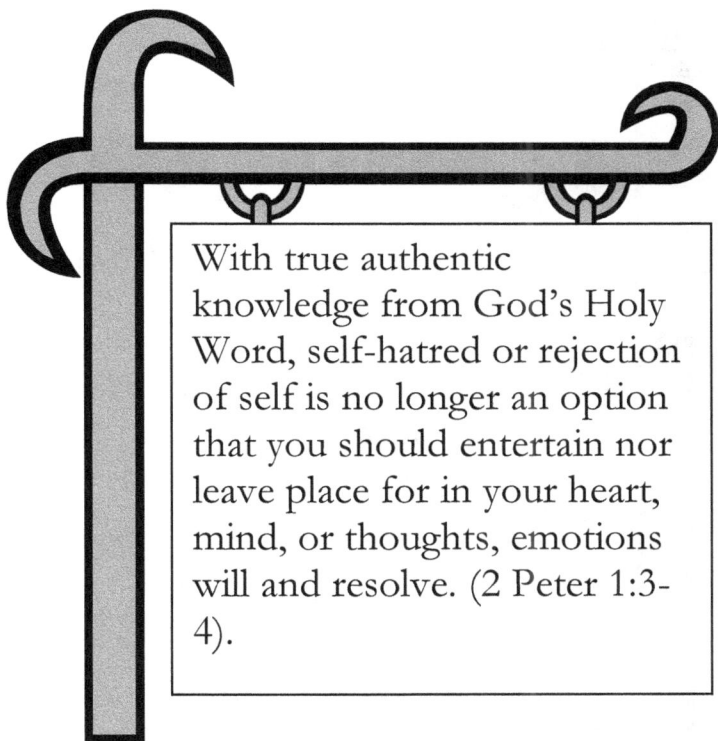

With true authentic knowledge from God's Holy Word, self-hatred or rejection of self is no longer an option that you should entertain nor leave place for in your heart, mind, or thoughts, emotions will and resolve. (2 Peter 1:3-4).

113

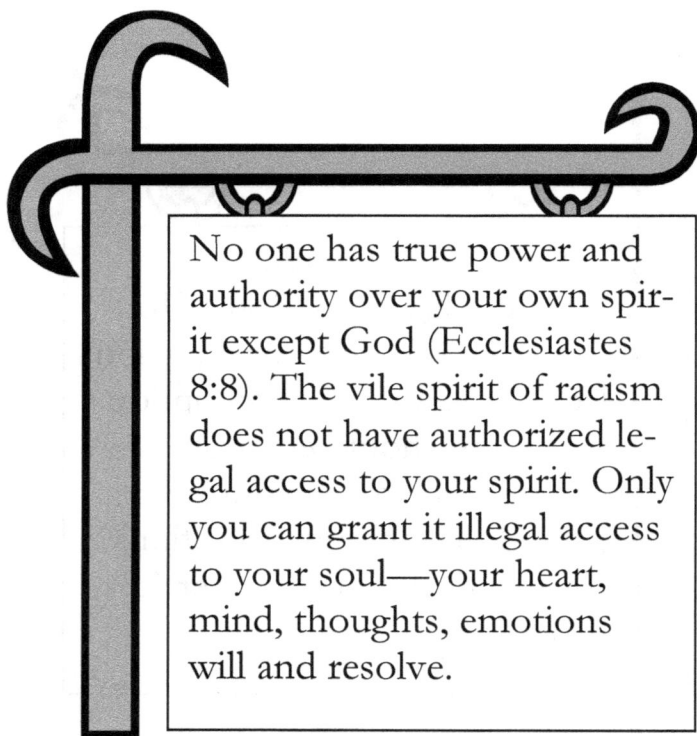

No one has true power and authority over your own spirit except God (Ecclesiastes 8:8). The vile spirit of racism does not have authorized legal access to your spirit. Only you can grant it illegal access to your soul—your heart, mind, thoughts, emotions will and resolve.

114

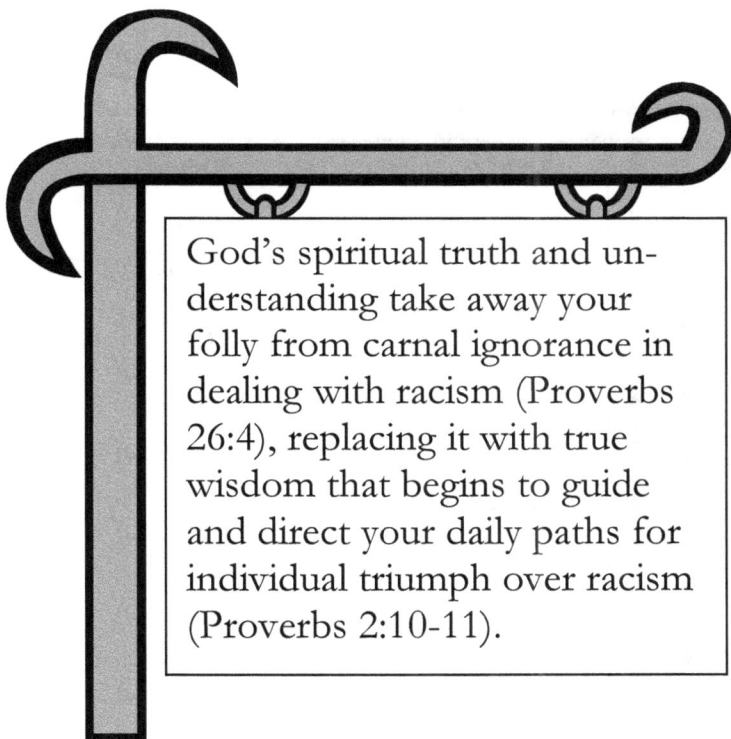

God's spiritual truth and understanding take away your folly from carnal ignorance in dealing with racism (Proverbs 26:4), replacing it with true wisdom that begins to guide and direct your daily paths for individual triumph over racism (Proverbs 2:10-11).

115

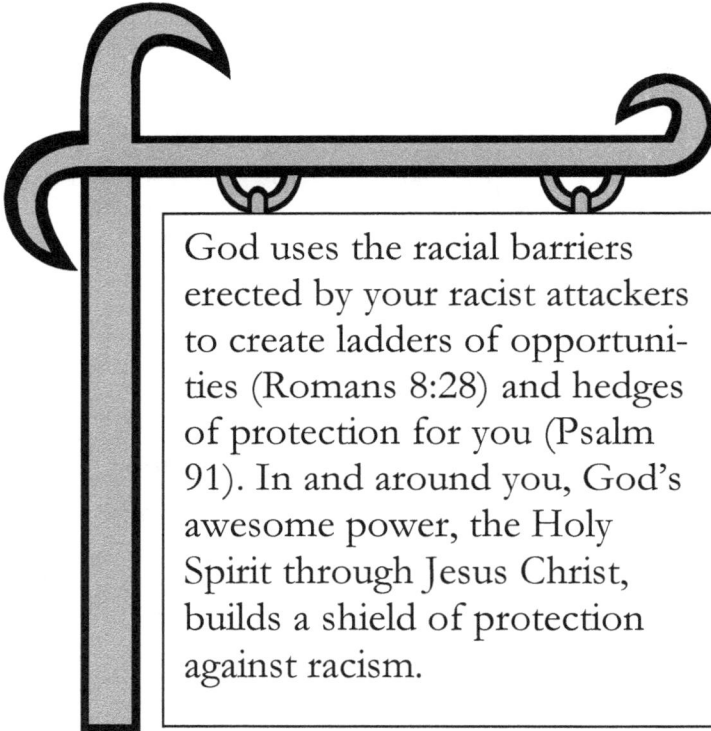

God uses the racial barriers erected by your racist attackers to create ladders of opportunities (Romans 8:28) and hedges of protection for you (Psalm 91). In and around you, God's awesome power, the Holy Spirit through Jesus Christ, builds a shield of protection against racism.

116

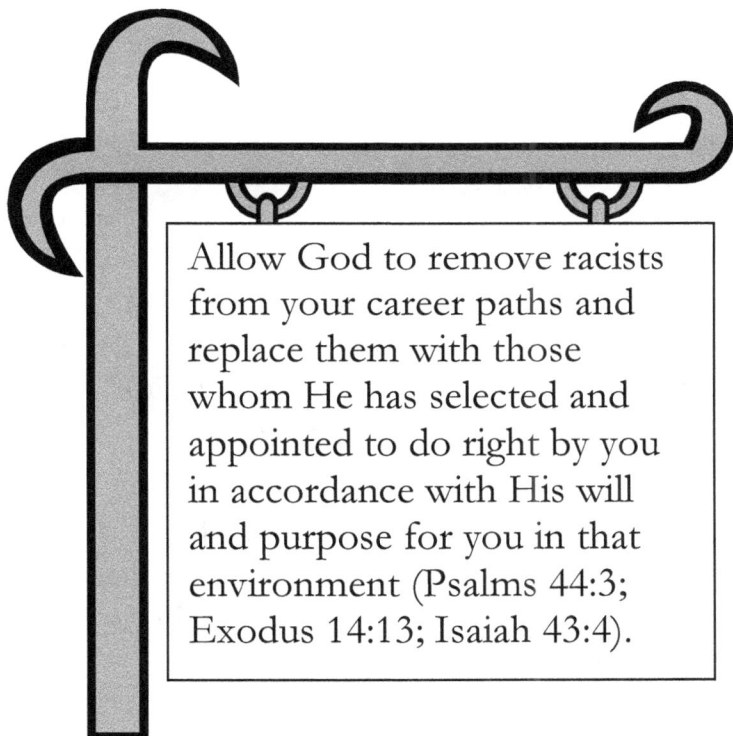

Allow God to remove racists from your career paths and replace them with those whom He has selected and appointed to do right by you in accordance with His will and purpose for you in that environment (Psalms 44:3; Exodus 14:13; Isaiah 43:4).

117

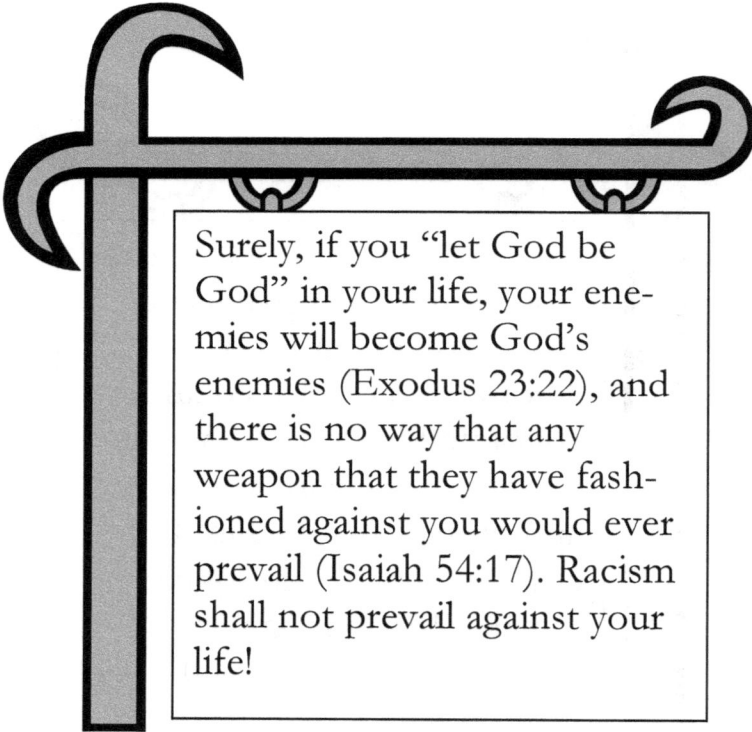

Surely, if you "let God be God" in your life, your enemies will become God's enemies (Exodus 23:22), and there is no way that any weapon that they have fashioned against you would ever prevail (Isaiah 54:17). Racism shall not prevail against your life!

118

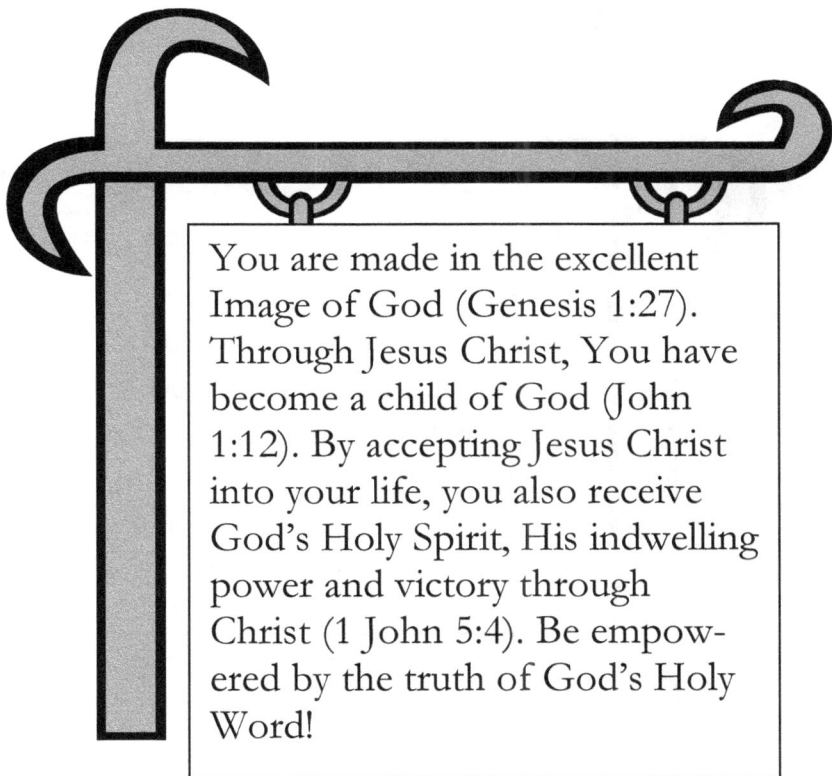

You are made in the excellent Image of God (Genesis 1:27). Through Jesus Christ, You have become a child of God (John 1:12). By accepting Jesus Christ into your life, you also receive God's Holy Spirit, His indwelling power and victory through Christ (1 John 5:4). Be empowered by the truth of God's Holy Word!

119

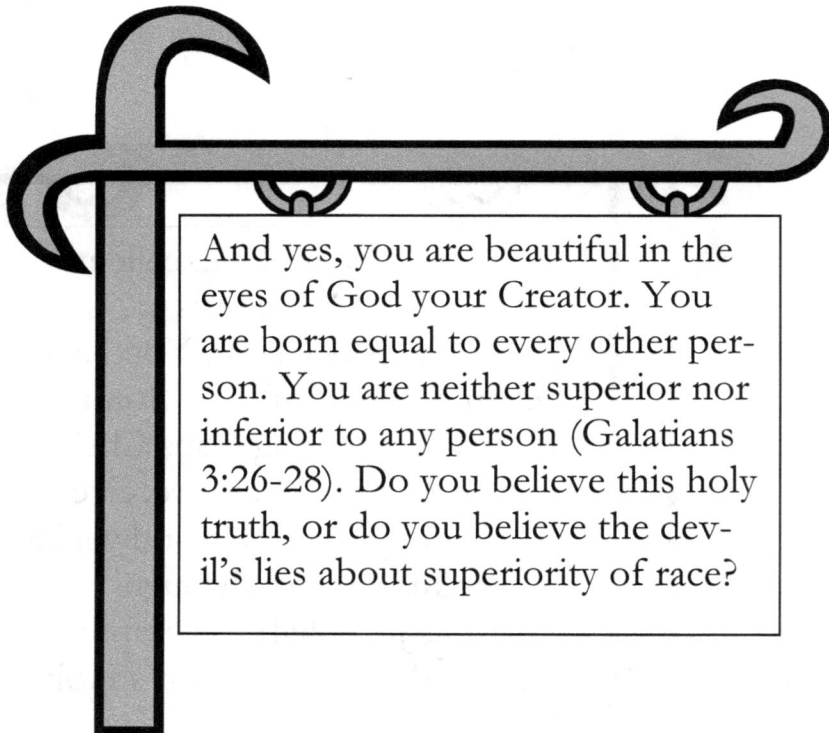

And yes, you are beautiful in the eyes of God your Creator. You are born equal to every other person. You are neither superior nor inferior to any person (Galatians 3:26-28). Do you believe this holy truth, or do you believe the devil's lies about superiority of race?

120

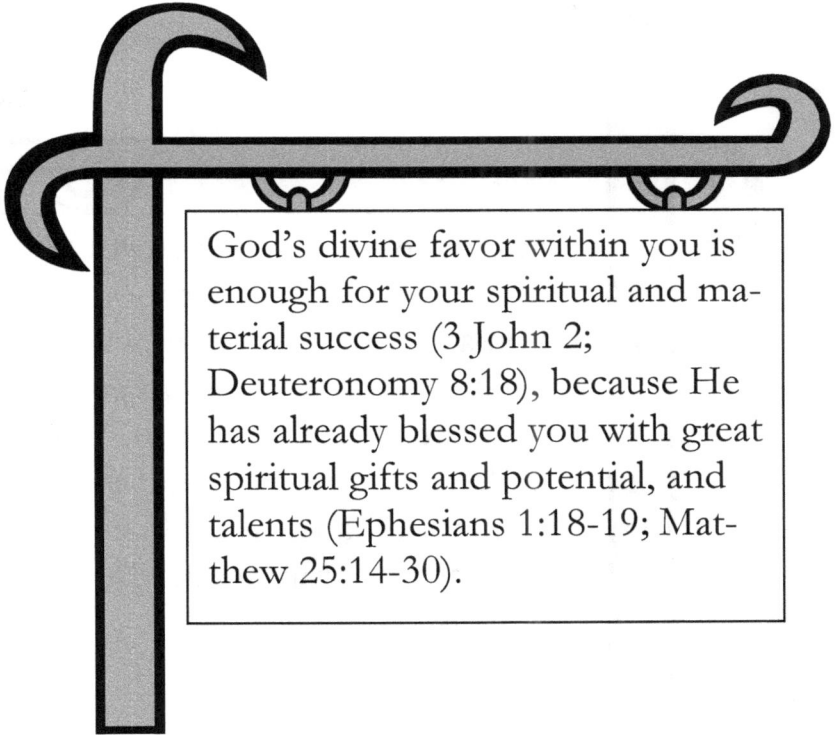

God's divine favor within you is enough for your spiritual and material success (3 John 2; Deuteronomy 8:18), because He has already blessed you with great spiritual gifts and potential, and talents (Ephesians 1:18-19; Matthew 25:14-30).

121

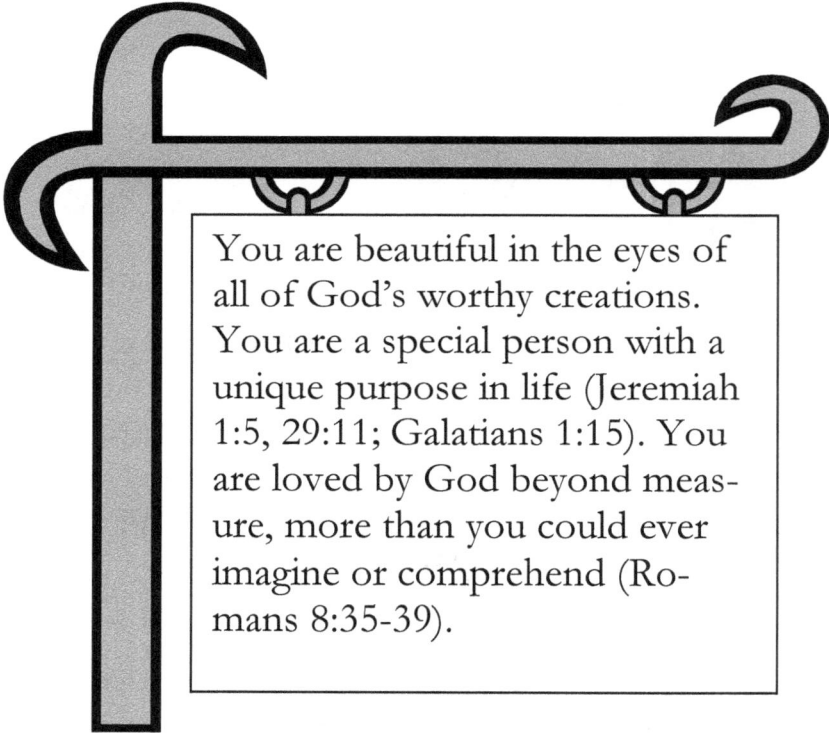

You are beautiful in the eyes of all of God's worthy creations. You are a special person with a unique purpose in life (Jeremiah 1:5, 29:11; Galatians 1:15). You are loved by God beyond measure, more than you could ever imagine or comprehend (Romans 8:35-39).

122

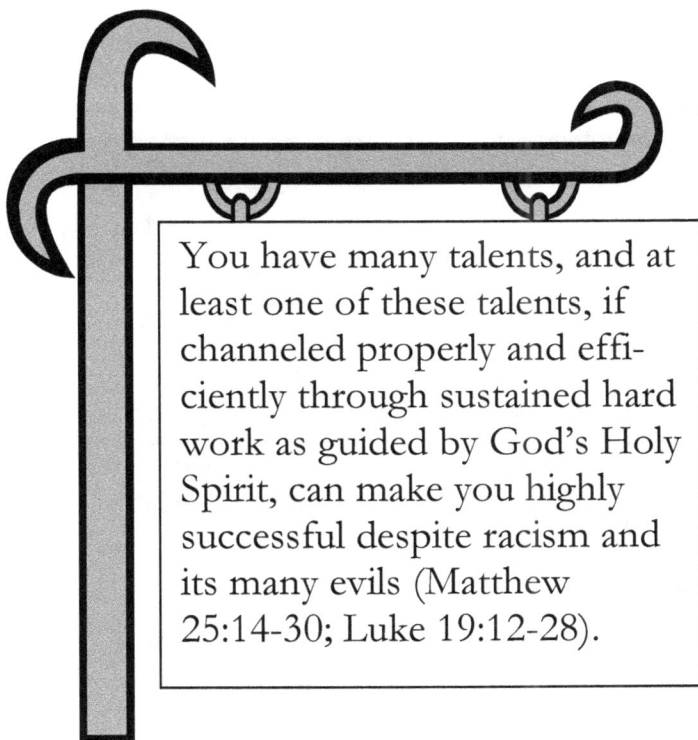

You have many talents, and at least one of these talents, if channeled properly and efficiently through sustained hard work as guided by God's Holy Spirit, can make you highly successful despite racism and its many evils (Matthew 25:14-30; Luke 19:12-28).

123

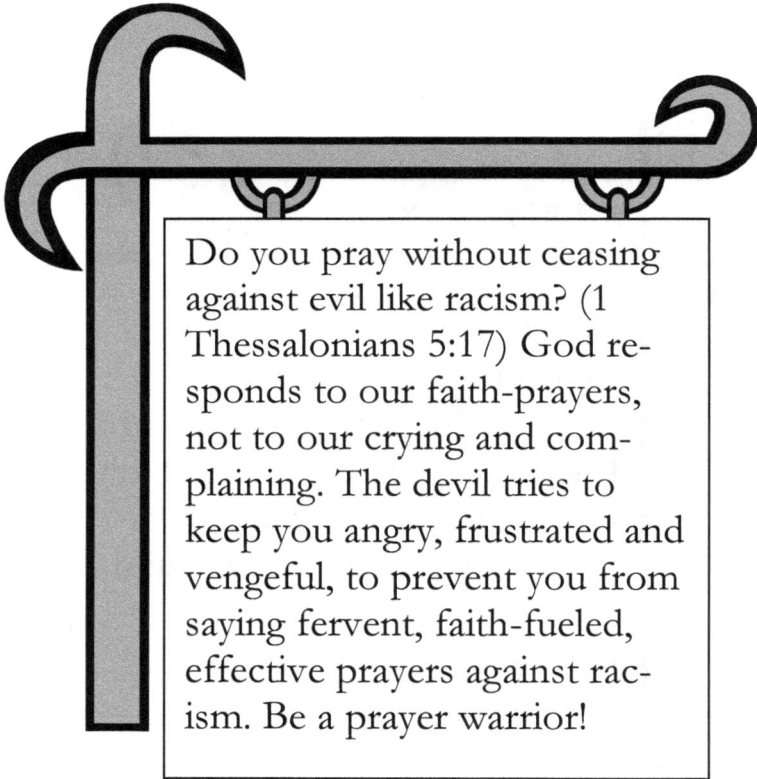

Do you pray without ceasing against evil like racism? (1 Thessalonians 5:17) God responds to our faith-prayers, not to our crying and complaining. The devil tries to keep you angry, frustrated and vengeful, to prevent you from saying fervent, faith-fueled, effective prayers against racism. Be a prayer warrior!

124

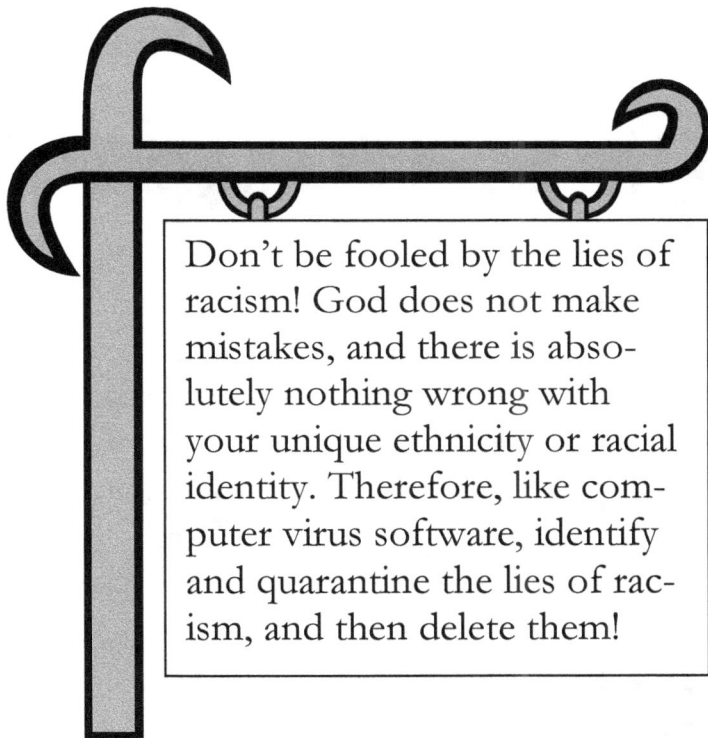

Don't be fooled by the lies of racism! God does not make mistakes, and there is absolutely nothing wrong with your unique ethnicity or racial identity. Therefore, like computer virus software, identify and quarantine the lies of racism, and then delete them!

125

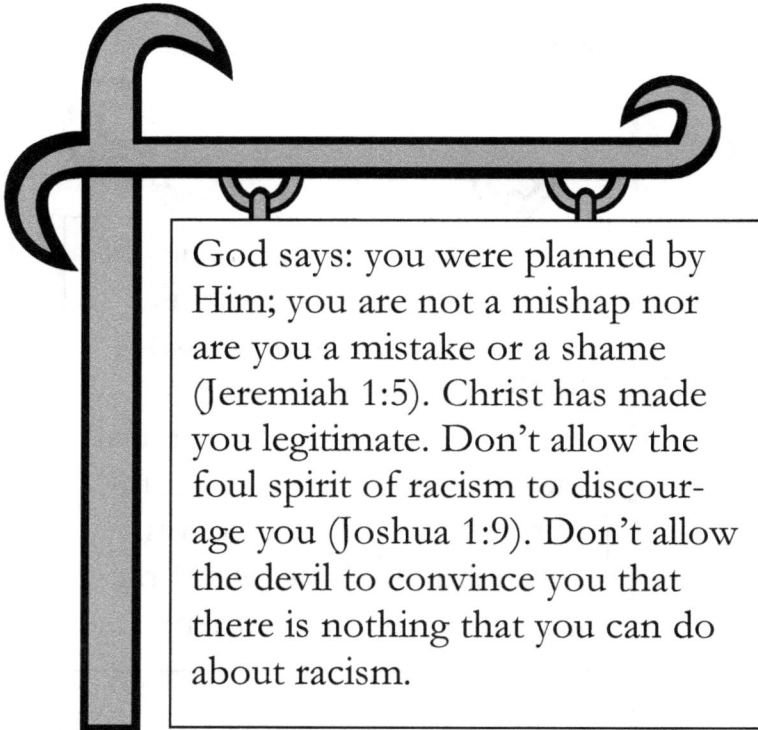

God says: you were planned by Him; you are not a mishap nor are you a mistake or a shame (Jeremiah 1:5). Christ has made you legitimate. Don't allow the foul spirit of racism to discourage you (Joshua 1:9). Don't allow the devil to convince you that there is nothing that you can do about racism.

126

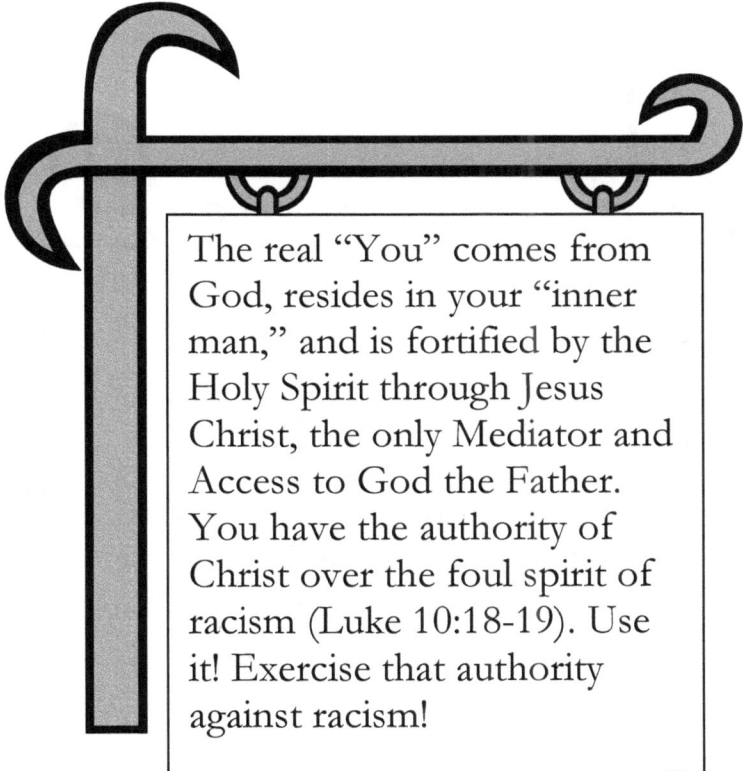

The real "You" comes from God, resides in your "inner man," and is fortified by the Holy Spirit through Jesus Christ, the only Mediator and Access to God the Father. You have the authority of Christ over the foul spirit of racism (Luke 10:18-19). Use it! Exercise that authority against racism!

127

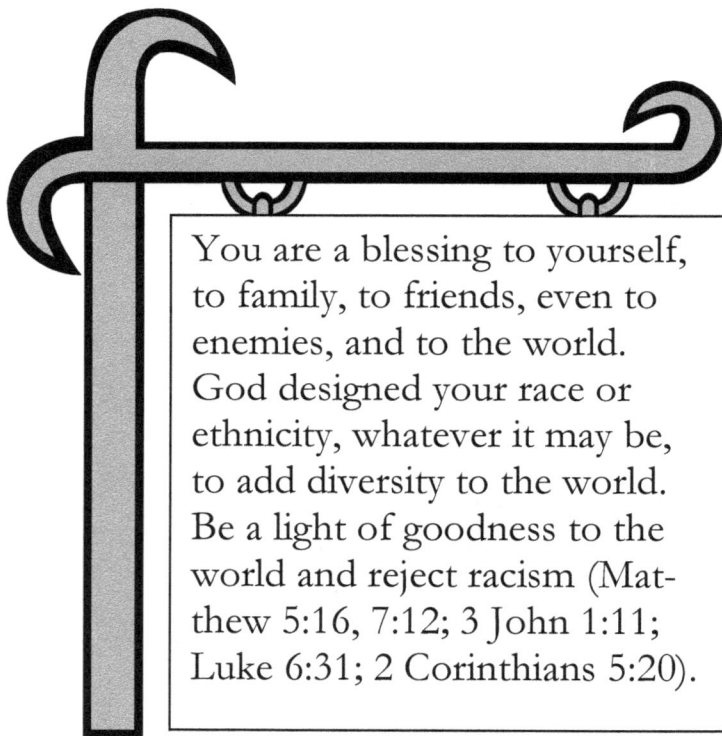

You are a blessing to yourself, to family, to friends, even to enemies, and to the world. God designed your race or ethnicity, whatever it may be, to add diversity to the world. Be a light of goodness to the world and reject racism (Matthew 5:16, 7:12; 3 John 1:11; Luke 6:31; 2 Corinthians 5:20).

128

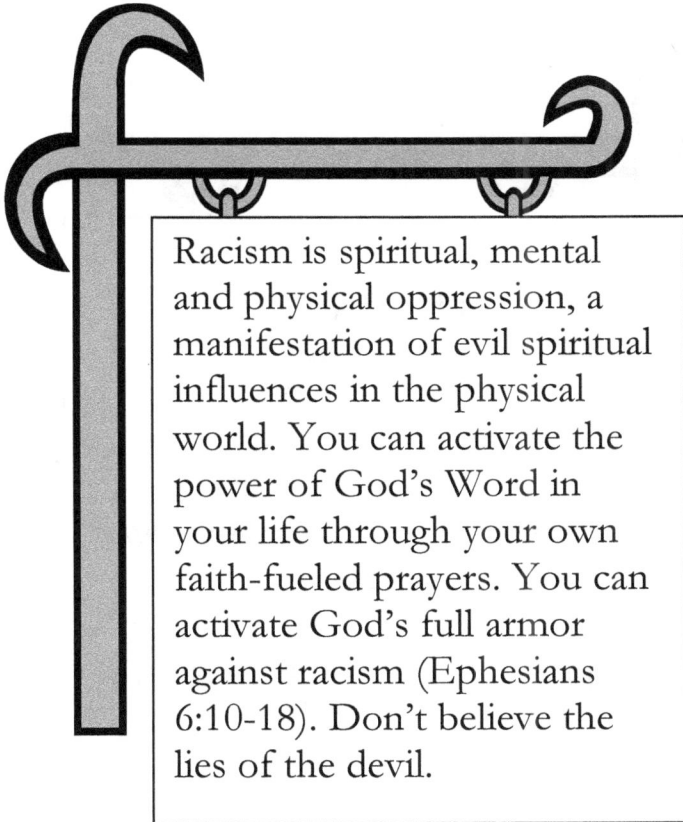

Racism is spiritual, mental and physical oppression, a manifestation of evil spiritual influences in the physical world. You can activate the power of God's Word in your life through your own faith-fueled prayers. You can activate God's full armor against racism (Ephesians 6:10-18). Don't believe the lies of the devil.

129

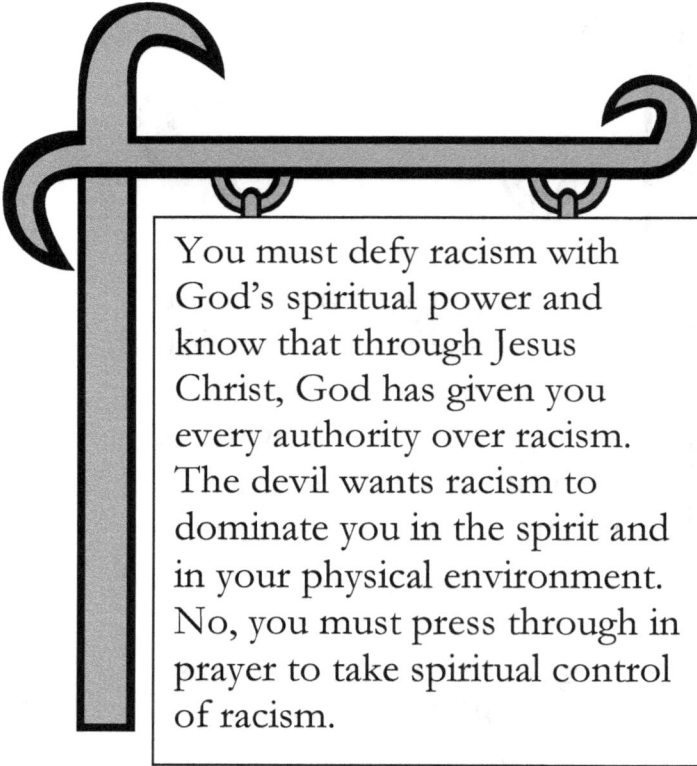

You must defy racism with God's spiritual power and know that through Jesus Christ, God has given you every authority over racism. The devil wants racism to dominate you in the spirit and in your physical environment. No, you must press through in prayer to take spiritual control of racism.

130

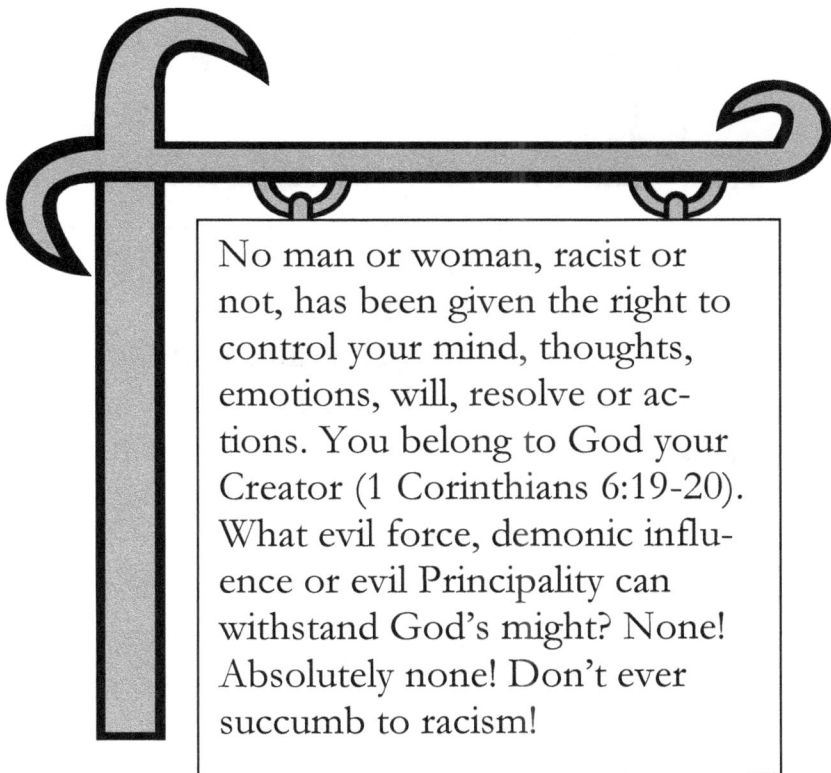

No man or woman, racist or not, has been given the right to control your mind, thoughts, emotions, will, resolve or actions. You belong to God your Creator (1 Corinthians 6:19-20). What evil force, demonic influence or evil Principality can withstand God's might? None! Absolutely none! Don't ever succumb to racism!

131

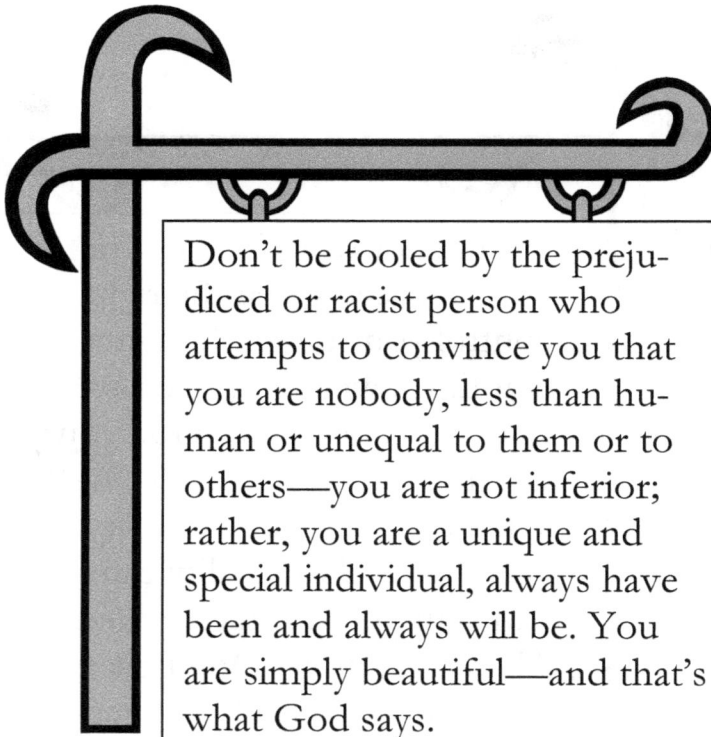

Don't be fooled by the prejudiced or racist person who attempts to convince you that you are nobody, less than human or unequal to them or to others—you are not inferior; rather, you are a unique and special individual, always have been and always will be. You are simply beautiful—and that's what God says.

132

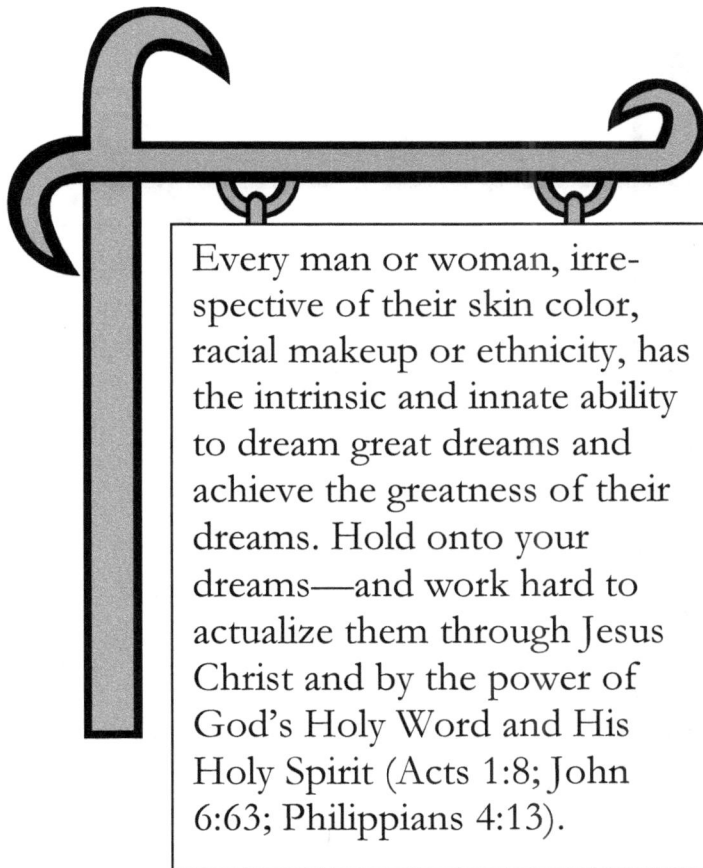

Every man or woman, irrespective of their skin color, racial makeup or ethnicity, has the intrinsic and innate ability to dream great dreams and achieve the greatness of their dreams. Hold onto your dreams—and work hard to actualize them through Jesus Christ and by the power of God's Holy Word and His Holy Spirit (Acts 1:8; John 6:63; Philippians 4:13).

133

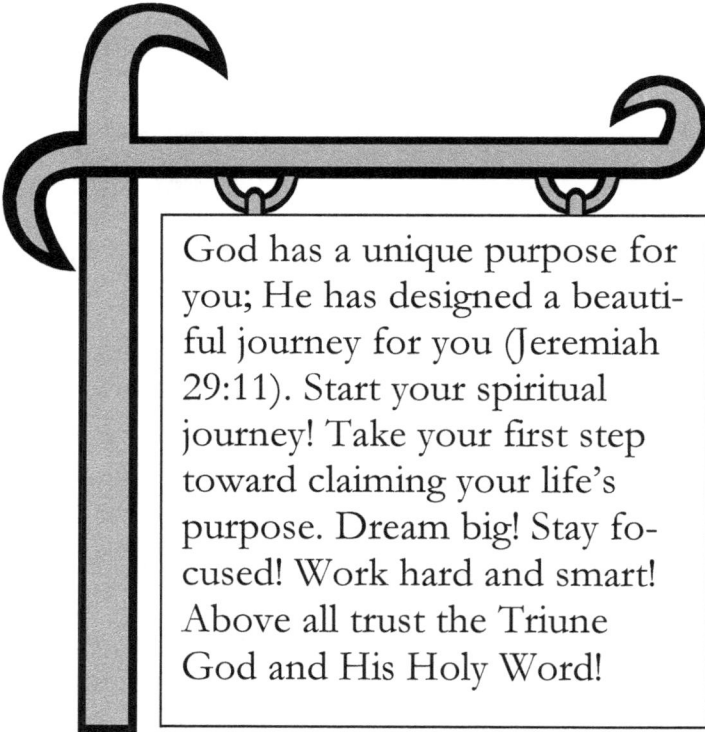

God has a unique purpose for you; He has designed a beautiful journey for you (Jeremiah 29:11). Start your spiritual journey! Take your first step toward claiming your life's purpose. Dream big! Stay focused! Work hard and smart! Above all trust the Triune God and His Holy Word!

134

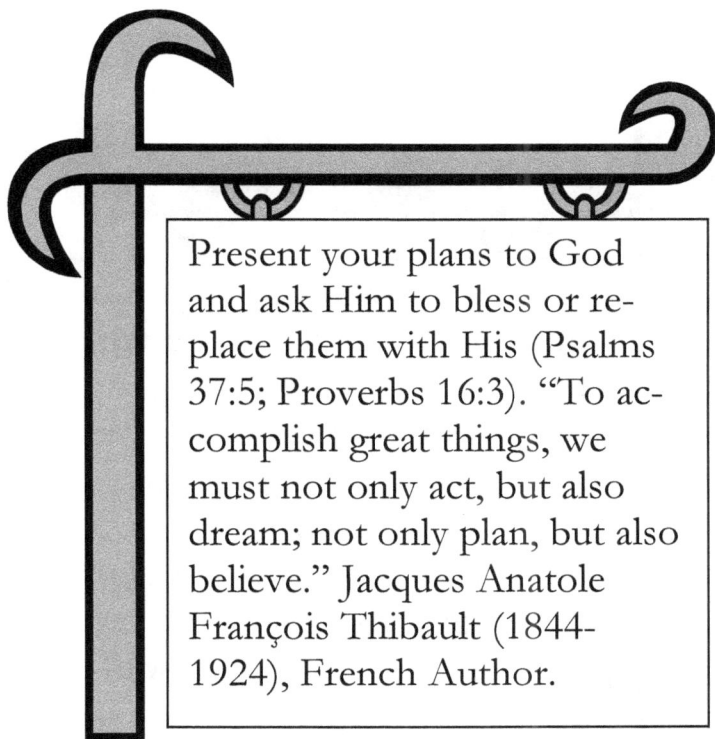

Present your plans to God and ask Him to bless or replace them with His (Psalms 37:5; Proverbs 16:3). "To accomplish great things, we must not only act, but also dream; not only plan, but also believe." Jacques Anatole François Thibault (1844-1924), French Author.

135

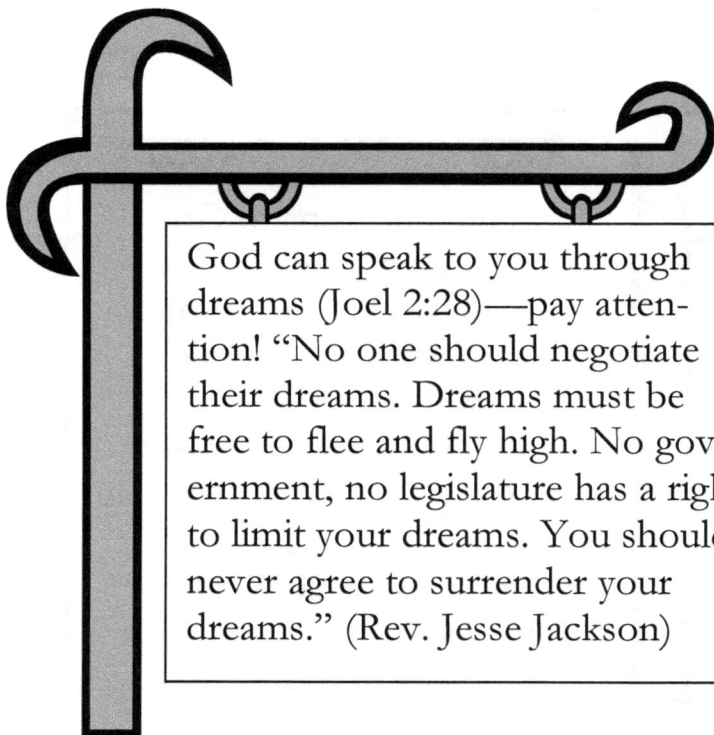

God can speak to you through dreams (Joel 2:28)—pay attention! "No one should negotiate their dreams. Dreams must be free to flee and fly high. No government, no legislature has a right to limit your dreams. You should never agree to surrender your dreams." (Rev. Jesse Jackson)

136

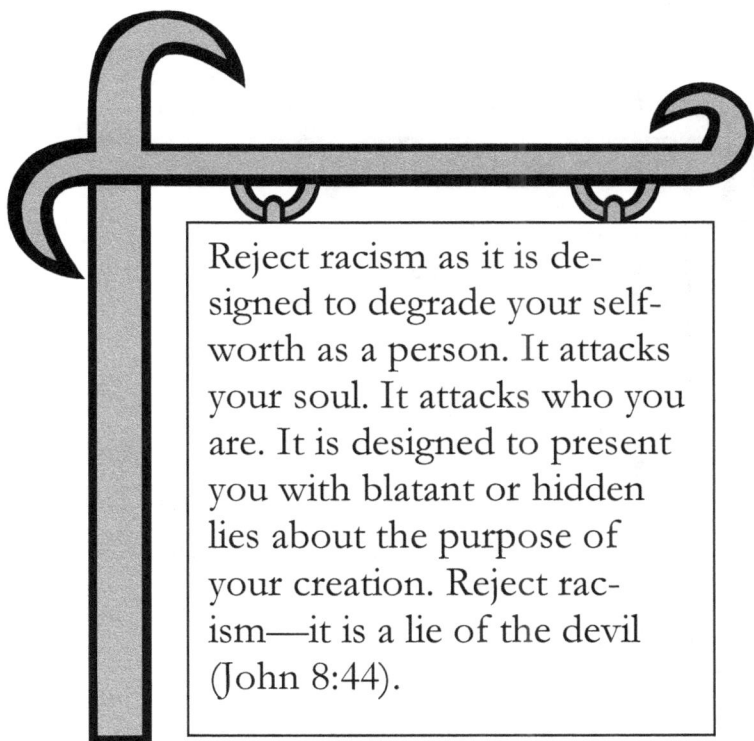

Reject racism as it is designed to degrade your self-worth as a person. It attacks your soul. It attacks who you are. It is designed to present you with blatant or hidden lies about the purpose of your creation. Reject racism—it is a lie of the devil (John 8:44).

137

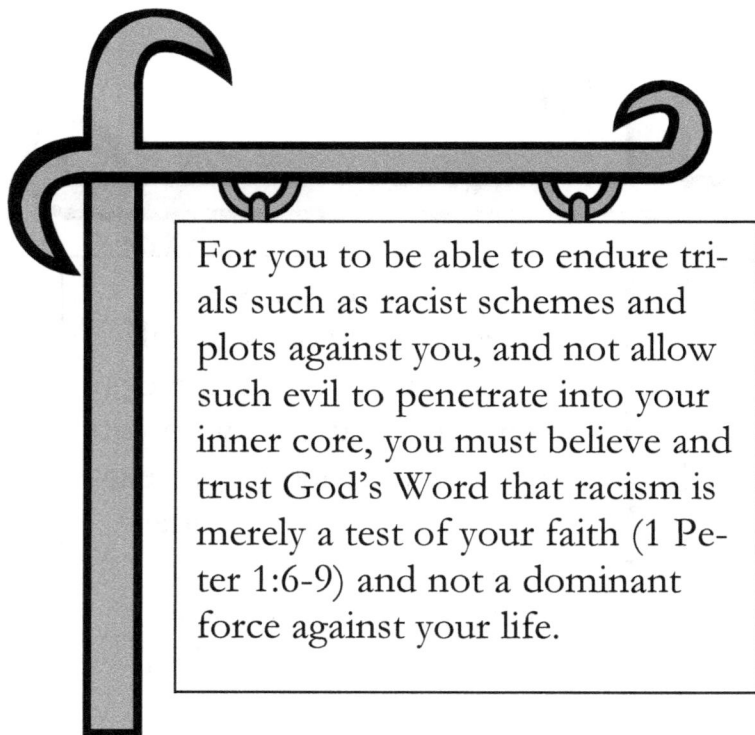

For you to be able to endure trials such as racist schemes and plots against you, and not allow such evil to penetrate into your inner core, you must believe and trust God's Word that racism is merely a test of your faith (1 Peter 1:6-9) and not a dominant force against your life.

138

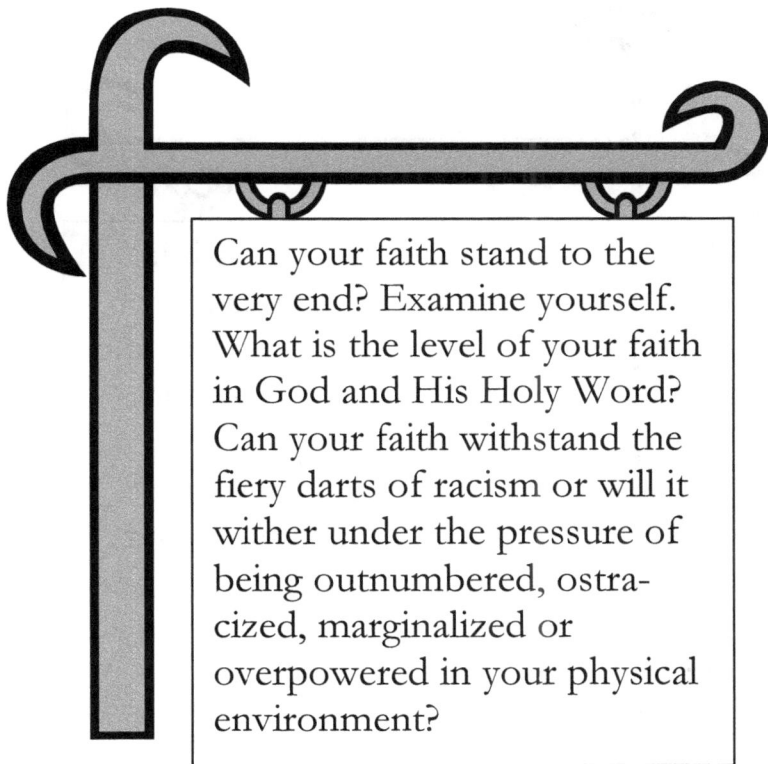

Can your faith stand to the very end? Examine yourself. What is the level of your faith in God and His Holy Word? Can your faith withstand the fiery darts of racism or will it wither under the pressure of being outnumbered, ostracized, marginalized or overpowered in your physical environment?

139

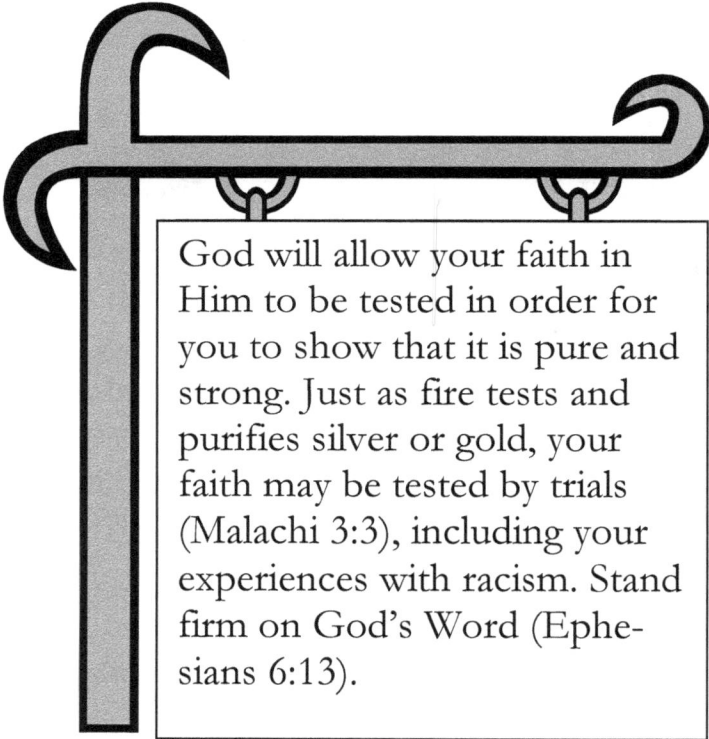

God will allow your faith in Him to be tested in order for you to show that it is pure and strong. Just as fire tests and purifies silver or gold, your faith may be tested by trials (Malachi 3:3), including your experiences with racism. Stand firm on God's Word (Ephesians 6:13).

140

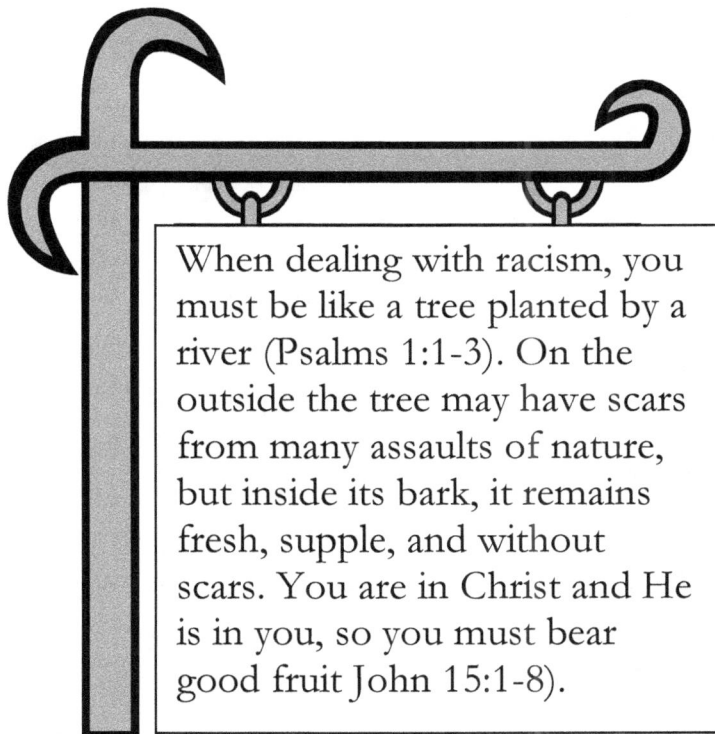

When dealing with racism, you must be like a tree planted by a river (Psalms 1:1-3). On the outside the tree may have scars from many assaults of nature, but inside its bark, it remains fresh, supple, and without scars. You are in Christ and He is in you, so you must bear good fruit John 15:1-8).

141

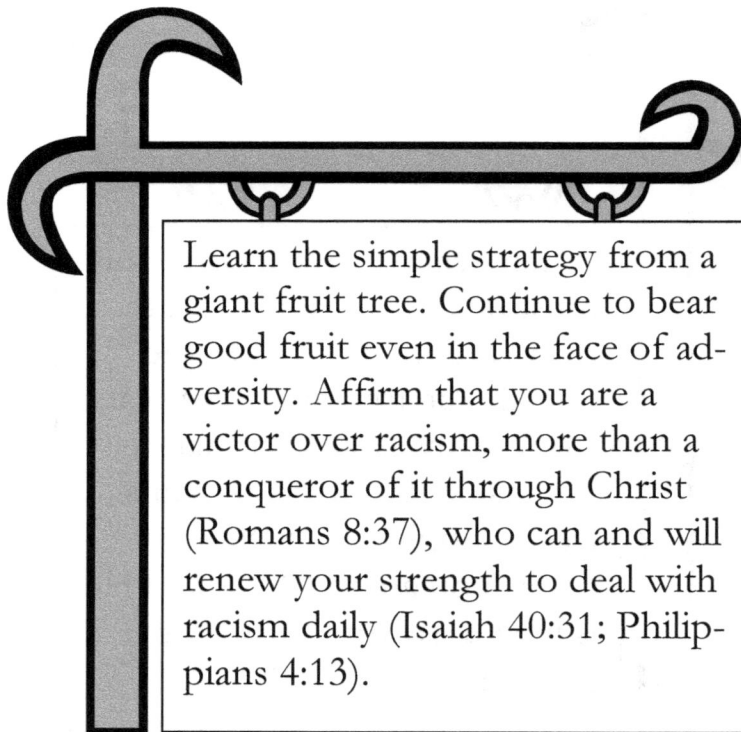

Learn the simple strategy from a giant fruit tree. Continue to bear good fruit even in the face of adversity. Affirm that you are a victor over racism, more than a conqueror of it through Christ (Romans 8:37), who can and will renew your strength to deal with racism daily (Isaiah 40:31; Philippians 4:13).

142

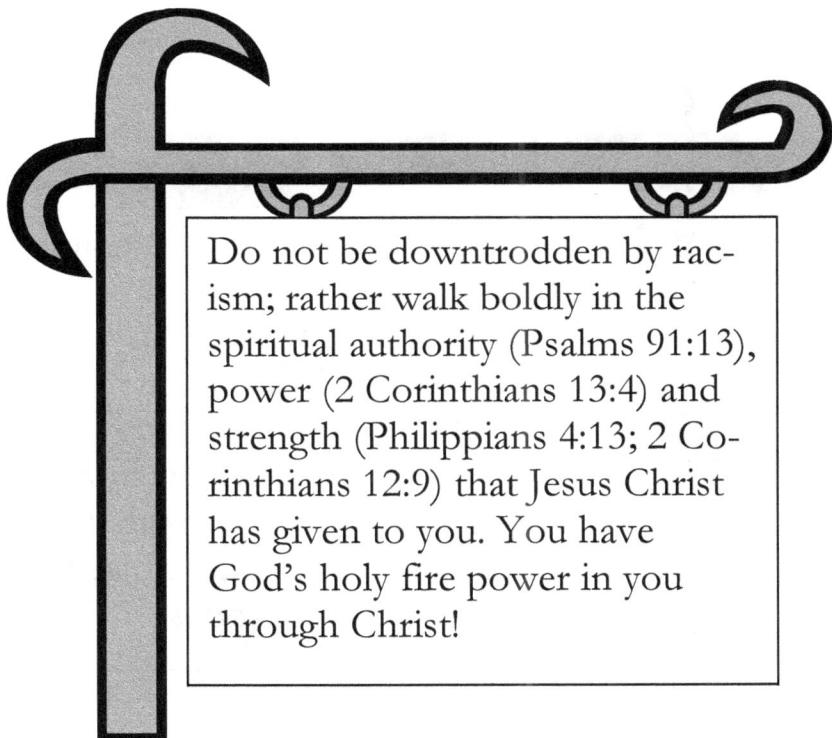

Do not be downtrodden by racism; rather walk boldly in the spiritual authority (Psalms 91:13), power (2 Corinthians 13:4) and strength (Philippians 4:13; 2 Corinthians 12:9) that Jesus Christ has given to you. You have God's holy fire power in you through Christ!

143

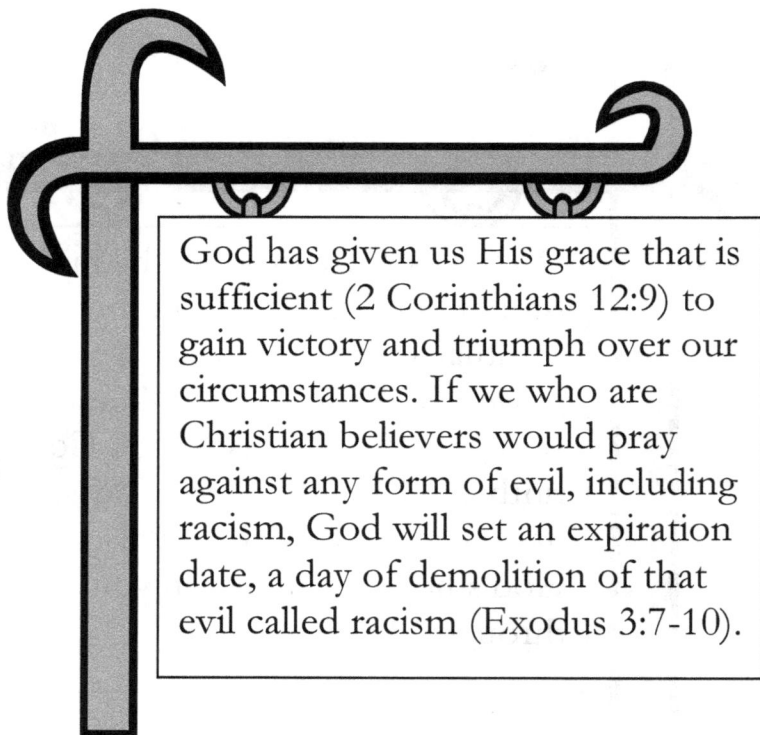

God has given us His grace that is sufficient (2 Corinthians 12:9) to gain victory and triumph over our circumstances. If we who are Christian believers would pray against any form of evil, including racism, God will set an expiration date, a day of demolition of that evil called racism (Exodus 3:7-10).

144

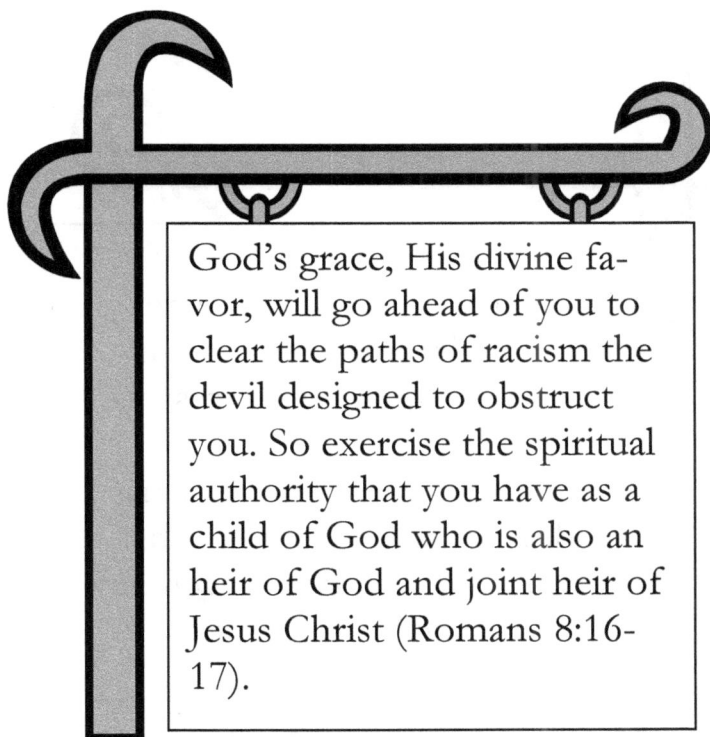

God's grace, His divine favor, will go ahead of you to clear the paths of racism the devil designed to obstruct you. So exercise the spiritual authority that you have as a child of God who is also an heir of God and joint heir of Jesus Christ (Romans 8:16-17).

145

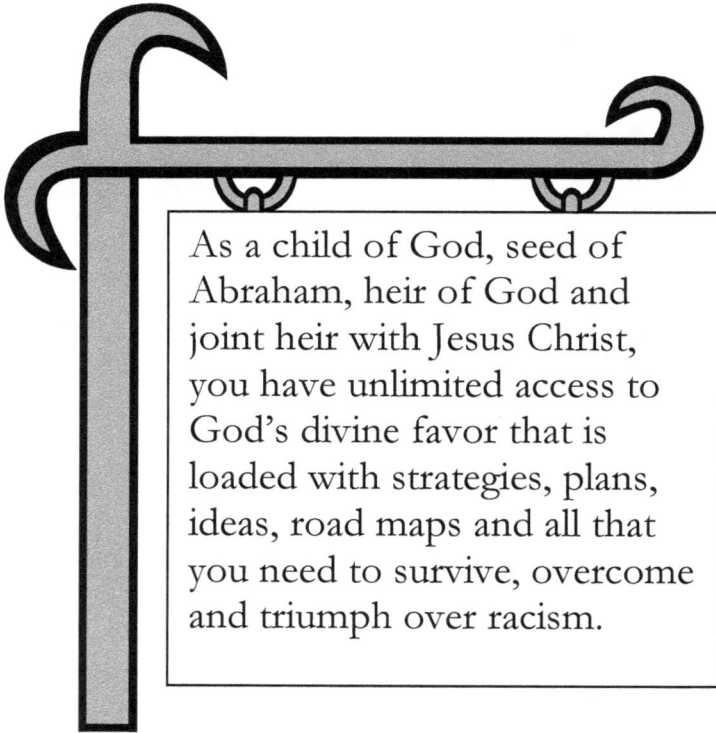

As a child of God, seed of Abraham, heir of God and joint heir with Jesus Christ, you have unlimited access to God's divine favor that is loaded with strategies, plans, ideas, road maps and all that you need to survive, overcome and triumph over racism.

146

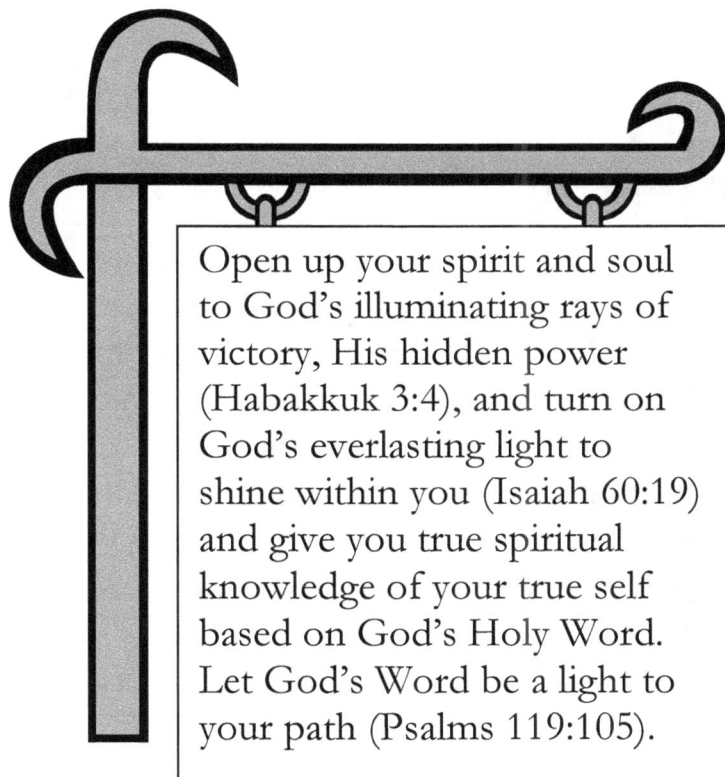

Open up your spirit and soul to God's illuminating rays of victory, His hidden power (Habakkuk 3:4), and turn on God's everlasting light to shine within you (Isaiah 60:19) and give you true spiritual knowledge of your true self based on God's Holy Word. Let God's Word be a light to your path (Psalms 119:105).

147

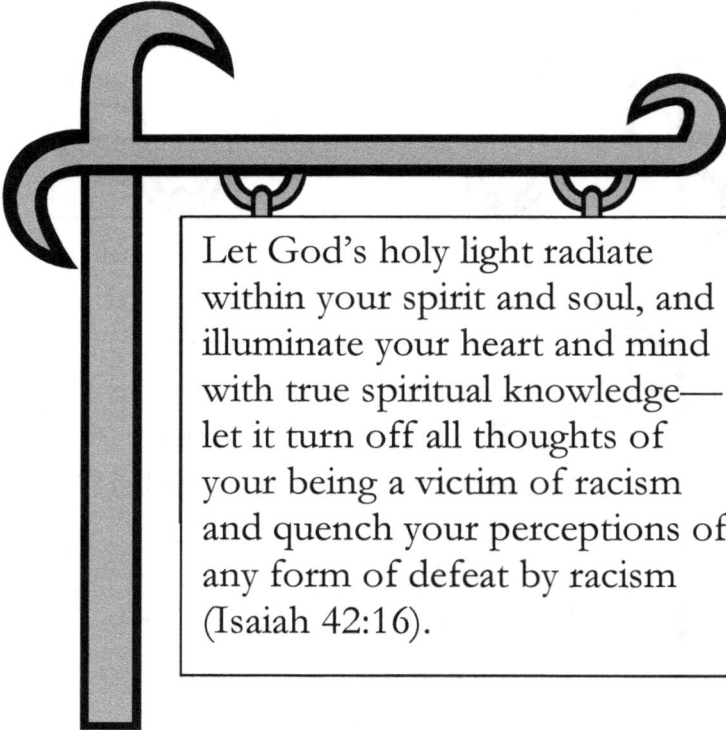

Let God's holy light radiate within your spirit and soul, and illuminate your heart and mind with true spiritual knowledge— let it turn off all thoughts of your being a victim of racism and quench your perceptions of any form of defeat by racism (Isaiah 42:16).

148

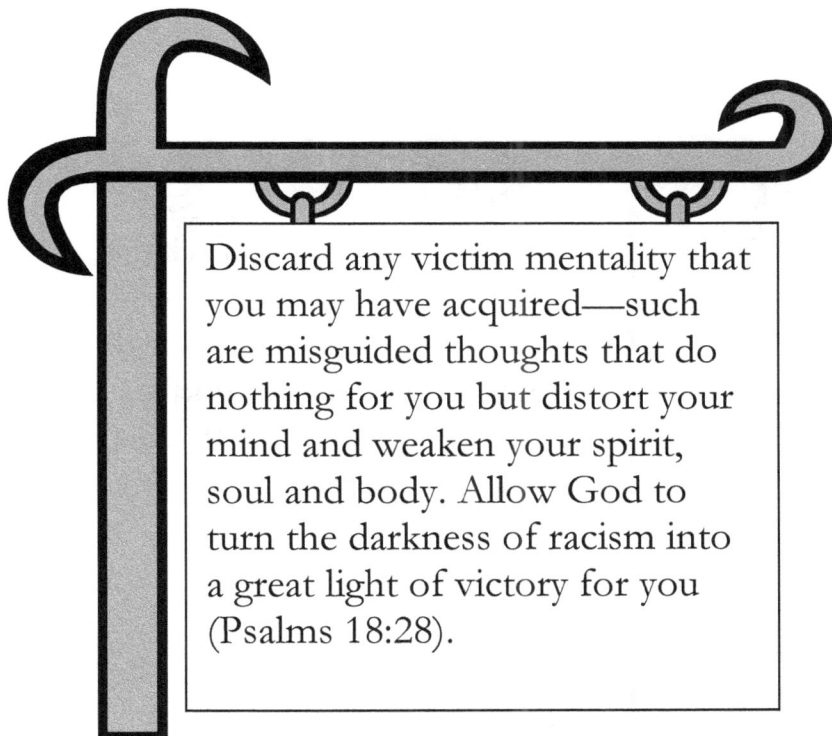

Discard any victim mentality that you may have acquired—such are misguided thoughts that do nothing for you but distort your mind and weaken your spirit, soul and body. Allow God to turn the darkness of racism into a great light of victory for you (Psalms 18:28).

149

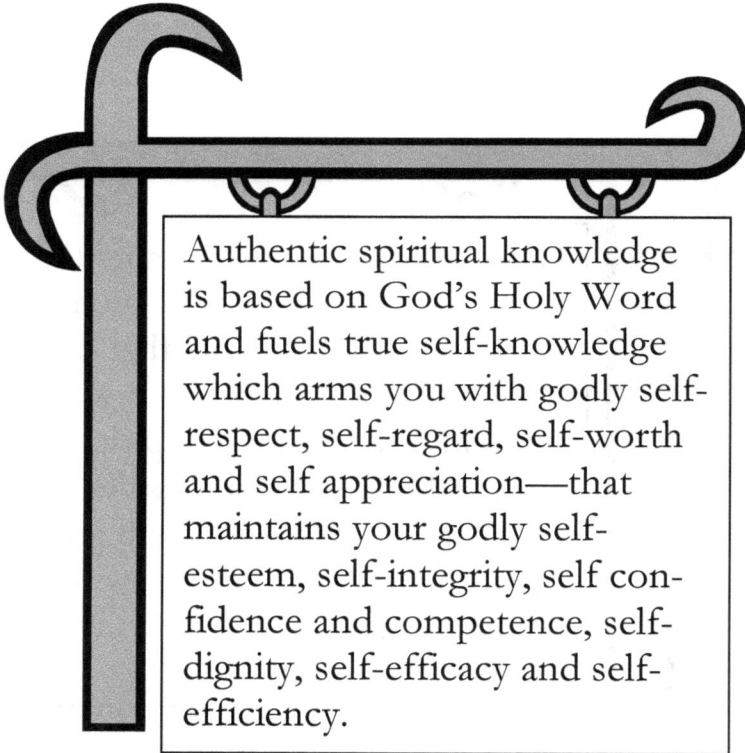

Authentic spiritual knowledge is based on God's Holy Word and fuels true self-knowledge which arms you with godly self-respect, self-regard, self-worth and self appreciation—that maintains your godly self-esteem, self-integrity, self confidence and competence, self-dignity, self-efficacy and self-efficiency.

150

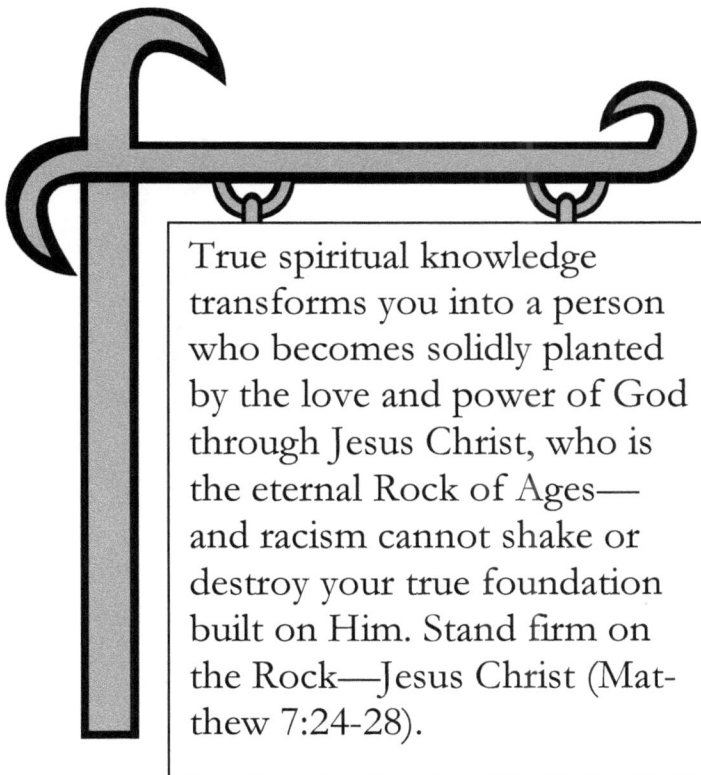

True spiritual knowledge transforms you into a person who becomes solidly planted by the love and power of God through Jesus Christ, who is the eternal Rock of Ages— and racism cannot shake or destroy your true foundation built on Him. Stand firm on the Rock—Jesus Christ (Matthew 7:24-28).

For whatever is born of God overcomes the world. And this is the victory that has overcome the world—our faith.

1 John 5:4

Available:
RAYS OF VICTORY SERIES

This Book:
150 SIGN POSTS TO VICTORY OVER RACISM

(Volume 2)

Empowering Sign posts for Victory Over Racism

∞∞∞∞∞∞∞∞∞∞ ♦ ♦ ♦ ♦ ♦ ∞∞∞∞∞∞∞∞∞∞

Excerpts from "Nailing Racism to the Cross"

∞∞∞∞∞∞∞∞∞∞ ♦ ♦ ♦ ♦ ♦ ∞∞∞∞∞∞∞∞∞∞

By
Dr. Jacyee Aniagolu-Johnson

First Paperback Edition
ISBN 978-1-937230-02-9

Also Available:
RAYS OF VICTORY SERIES

150 SIGN POSTS TO VICTORY OVER RACISM

(Volume 1)

Empowering Sign posts for Victory Over Racism

∞∞∞∞∞∞∞∞∞∞ ♦ ♦ ♦ ♦ ♦ ∞∞∞∞∞∞∞∞∞∞

Excerpts from "Nailing Racism to the Cross"

∞∞∞∞∞∞∞∞∞∞ ♦ ♦ ♦ ♦ ♦ ∞∞∞∞∞∞∞∞∞∞

By
Dr. Jacyee Aniagolu-Johnson

First Paperback Edition
ISBN 978-1-937230-01-2

RAYS OF VICTORY SERIES

150 SIGN POSTS TO VICTORY OVER RACISM

(Volume 3)

Empowering Sign posts for Victory Over Racism

∞∞∞∞∞∞∞∞∞ ♦ ♦ ♦ ♦ ♦ ∞∞∞∞∞∞∞∞∞

Excerpts from "Nailing Racism to the Cross"

∞∞∞∞∞∞∞∞∞ ♦ ♦ ♦ ♦ ♦ ∞∞∞∞∞∞∞∞∞

By
Dr. Jacyee Aniagolu-Johnson

First Paperback Edition
ISBN 978-1-937230-03-6

RAYS OF VICTORY SERIES

POWER THOUGHTS AGAINST RACISM

Power of a Christ-rooted Mindset Over Racism

∞∞∞∞∞∞∞∞∞ ♦ ♦ ♦ ♦ ♦ ∞∞∞∞∞∞∞∞∞

Excerpts from "Nailing Racism to the Cross"

∞∞∞∞∞∞∞∞∞ ♦ ♦ ♦ ♦ ♦ ∞∞∞∞∞∞∞∞∞

By
Dr. Jacyee Aniagolu-Johnson

First Paperback Edition
ISBN 978-1-937230-00-5

RAYS OF VICTORY SERIES

POWER THOUGHTS

Diary

FOR VICTORY OVER RACISM

Journal for Power Thoughts Against Racism
[With Excerpts from "Nailing Racism to the Cross"]

By
Dr. Jacyee Aniagolu-Johnson

First Paperback Edition:
ISBN: 978-1-937230-04-3

RAYS OF VICTORY SERIES

WORKBOOK SERIES

FOOTPRINTS OF VICTORY OVER RACISM

In the Secret Place With God
(Volume 1)

Illuminating Daily Guideposts for God's Rays of Victory Over Racism

By
Dr. Jacyee Aniagolu-Johnson

First Paperback Edition
ISBN 978-0-9789669-5-9

RAYS OF VICTORY SERIES

WORKBOOK SERIES

FOOTPRINTS OF VICTORY OVER RACISM

In the Secret Place With God (Volume 2)

Illuminating Daily Guideposts for God's Rays of Victory Over Racism

By
Dr. Jacyee Aniagolu-Johnson

First Paperback Edition
ISBN 978-0-9789669-6-6

RAYS OF VICTORY SERIES

ON THE HAMMOCK:
WITH THE SWORD OF THE SPIRIT

FOR INDIVIDUAL VICTORY OVER RACISM

A Meditation Journal
[40 Days of Daily Meditation]
(Volume 1)

By
Dr. Jacyee Aniagolu-Johnson

First Paperback Edition
ISBN 978-0-9789669-8-0

RAYS OF VICTORY SERIES

ON THE HAMMOCK:
WITH THE OIL OF GRACE

FOR INDIVIDUAL VICTORY OVER RACISM

A Meditation Journal
[40 Days of Daily Meditation]
(Volume 2)

By

Dr. Jacyee Aniagolu-Johnson

First Paperback Edition
ISBN 978-0-9789669-9-7

RAYS OF VICTORY SERIES

ONE ON ONE WITH GOD

FOR VICTORY OVER RACISM

Daily Prayer Conversations With God for Individual Victory Over Racism

By

Dr. Jacyee Aniagolu-Johnson

First Paperback Edition:
ISBN 978-0-9789669-7-3

RAYS OF VICTORY SERIES

My Rays of Victory

BIBLE STUDY DIARY

A Unique Diary for your Signature Penmanship as you Triumph Over Racism

By

Dr. Jacyee Aniagolu-Johnson

First Paperback Edition:
ISBN: 978-0-9789669-4-2

Rays of Victory Series

Correspondence:

Please send Correspondence to:

Marble Tower Publishing

P.O. Box 1654, Laurel, Maryland 20725

OR

Submit a Contact Request Form at:

www.marbletowerpublishing.com

www.ravbookseries.com

www.ingramcontent.com/pod-product-compliance
Lightning Source LLC
Chambersburg PA
CBHW071122280326
41935CB00010B/1088